MESSAGES

MESSAGES

EVIDENCE FOR LIFE AFTER DEATH

George E. Dalzell, L.C.S.W.

HAMPTON ROADS
PUBLISHING COMPANY, INC.

for the evolving human spirit

Lola
Words and music by Frederick Hollander
Copyright © 1955 (Renewed 1983) by Famous Music Corporation
International Copyright Secured   All Rights Reserved
Used by permission.

Get Here by Brenda Russell
Copyright © 1988, 1991
WB Music Corporation and Rutland Road Music
All rights administered by WB Music Corporation,
All rights reserved. Used by permission.
Warner Brothers Publications U.S., Inc.
Miami, FL 33014

Cover design by Marjoram Productions
Cover art copyright © by Digital Vision

Hampton Roads Publishing Company, Inc.
1125 Stoney Ridge Road
Charlottesville, VA 22902

434-296-2772
fax: 434-296-5096
e-mail: hrpc@hrpub.com
www.hrpub.com

If you are unable to order this book from your local
bookseller, you may order directly from the publisher.
Call 1-800-766-8009, toll-free.

Library of Congress Catalog Card Number: 2001098008

ISBN 1-57174-296-4

10 9 8 7 6 5 4 3 2

Printed on acid-free paper in Canada

Dedication

For Ludwig and Annabel,

Brian Hurst, and Lena

Contents

Foreword

Evidence-Based Mediumship

You are about to read an inspiring book that describes the journey of a courageous and caring social worker and evidence-based medium, George E. Dalzell, who has obtained compelling data that his deceased friend, Michael Keller, is still alive.

When I first met George in Palm Springs in February 2000, I was immediately impressed by his honesty and openness. Here was a psychiatric social worker in Los Angeles County who was willing to put his professional career on the line for his strong convictions about mediumship science. He was preparing to share his personal story, addressing one of the most important and controversial questions in contemporary science and religion—the possibility of survival of consciousness after physical death. George was practicing what we term "evidence-based mediumship," which follows the same scientific standards as evidence-based medicine.

Based on our on-going scientific research with a dream

team of "Michael Jordans" of the mediumship world (including John Edward, Laurie Campbell, Suzanne Northrop, Anne Gehmen, and George Anderson), we say the following:

"If mediums are willing to stand up and be counted, scientists should be willing to stand up and count them."

However, it's one thing to be a practicing medium and risk your career in mediumship itself; it's quite another to be a practicing health care professional and risk the rejection of your colleagues.

I know what it is like to put one's career on the line by "letting the data speak." I am a professor of psychology, medicine, neurology, psychiatry, and surgery, and director of the Human Energy Systems Laboratory (HESL) at the University of Arizona. The laboratory integrates mind-body medicine, energy medicine, and spiritual medicine. The research conducted in the laboratory involves testing the survival-of-consciousness hypothesis. The rationale for this work is described in my book with Linda G. Russek, Ph.D., *The Living Energy Universe* (Hampton Roads, 1999).

When I learned of George's professional history and the sequence of events that led him to collect convincing evidence of Michael Keller's continued existence, I was excited yet skeptical. Scientists are typically a conservative group. Scientists prefer to sit on the fence rather than take a side, one way or the other. I was trained to think that way. For example, concerning the survival-of-consciousness hypothesis, it is more conservative to say things like "the data suggest that survival may be true," rather than say definitively that "there is no evidence for survival" (the negative conclusion), or "the data convincingly indicate that survival exists" (the positive conclusion).

Well-trained scientists are skilled in sitting on fences. However, what you are about to read provides more than just a strong rationale to come down off the fence. In fact, the latest experiment, with the apparent collaboration of Michael Keller, conducted after *Messages* was completed, provided evidence of Michael's continued existence that pushed us off the fence. Evidence was obtained by a research medium that even author George Dalzell himself did not know.

Being Pushed Off the Fence—Receiving Definitive Information Long Distance Before Talking with the Sitter

Here is a thumbnail sketch of the experiment.

It was December 17th, 2000. The chair of our mediumship research committee, Laurie Campbell, was in Tucson for a unique experiment. She was scheduled to conduct long-distance research readings by telephone with people she did not know. Hence, Laurie was "blind" to whom the sitters would be. George was invited to be one of the sitters and was scheduled for 6:00 P.M.

At 5:30 PM., Laurie went into seclusion. This was a pre-reading meditation, during which Laurie attempted to receive information from the deceased loved ones *before the reading actually began.* Sitters were told a day before their scheduled readings were to take place that pre-reading meditation periods would occur immediately prior to their scheduled appointments and that they should invite their deceased loved ones to come early.

Linda Russek and I (but not Laurie) knew that George would invite Michael to come early. However, we were blind as to the names and relationships of other people George chose to invite as well. It is also important to note that we didn't share the manuscript for *Messages* with Laurie Campbell, nor did we discuss any aspect of George Dalzell's experiences at any time prior to the experiment.

At 6:00 P.M., I called George. Laurie was kept blind to George's identity, including his name, gender, etc. I reminded George that the first ten or so minutes would be conducted in silence and that I would put the phone on mute and then hand the phone to Laurie. Hence, George did not hear what Laurie was receiving and saying out loud during the silent-sitter period. This information was recorded on a Sony digital video camera.

At approximately 6:15, I took the phone off mute, and Laurie was allowed to speak with George for the first time. Since Laurie and George had never met in person or spoken by telephone, Laurie did not recognize George's voice. However, George recognized Laurie's voice because he had seen her participate in our laboratory research featured on HBO's special, *Life Afterlife*, and A&E's special, *Beyond Death*.

After Laurie introduced herself, she reviewed with George what she had received during the pre-reading meditation period. For the purpose of this experiment, George was to be kept blind to what was said during the silent-sitter muted phone period.

Are you ready to learn who George invited to serve in the roles of "departed hypothesized co-investigators," and what information Laurie received before she and George *ever spoke*?

George invited his friend Michael, his aunt Alice, his father, Bob, and his friend Jerry, recently deceased.

Laurie received specific information that:

1. the reading was for a male sitter named George (true);
2. the primary deceased person was a dear partner named Michael (true);
3. there was a deceased person named Alice (true);
4. there was a deceased person named Bob (true);
5. there was a deceased friend named Jerry (true);
6. there was a friend named "Talya" (true) (Laurie's spelling);
7. there was a small deceased dog belonging to George with "an *S* name near water and a tree" (true) (George's small deceased dog, whose name began with an *S* (Sonya), was buried by a large oak tree at the Dalzell family cottage directly on Lake Erie).

In the scientific paper we wrote on this research reading (Schwartz and Russek, 2001), we calculated that the probability of Laurie getting this information about Michael and George's other friends and family correct by chance alone was less than one in 2.6 trillion.

But that's not all.

During the actual reading—when Laurie could talk to George—Laurie received four pieces of information that George himself did not know and confirmed later by calling Michael's family, George's family, and friends:

1. Michael showed Laurie a "monastery-like place" of "century-old stones" near the river on the way to his home in the country. George called Michael's family, who live in Kirschfurt, Germany, and discovered not only that an old church is beside the river Main on the way to their home, but that they

had held a service for Michael at this very church a few weeks before the experiment was conducted.

2. Aunt Alice told Laurie that she was experiencing sorrow and concern for her granddaughter, Katherine, who was "out of control" and receiving some kind of "healing." George called Katherine's mother and learned that her daughter was indeed having trouble and had sought psychological counseling a week before the experiment.

3. George was convinced that Laurie had spelled Katherine's name wrong. He believed that the correct spelling was Catherine. To his surprise (and ours), he later learned that Laurie had got it right.

4. Jerry showed Laurie that he had lived on the East Coast, in Brooklyn. George called one of Jerry's friends and learned that Jerry had lived in Brooklyn, New York, before moving to Manhattan, where later he met George.

Most importantly for George, the "live" reading provided continued confirmation in the lab that Michael Keller, the subject of *Messages,* appeared willing and able to act as a spirit collaborator in the experiment. He "showed up." As you'll read in the pages to come, this was one in a series of attempts in which George endeavored to make contact with Michael via mediumship, with the ultimate purpose of consoling his bereaved family.

William James, M.D., the distinguished professor at Harvard University approximately one hundred years ago, said, "In order to disprove the law that all crows are black, it is enough to find one white crow." Laurie and George appear to be two "white-crow" mediums, and their laboratory session can be called a "white-crow" research reading.

Celebrating the Mind and the Living Soul

Messages is a book that celebrates how the human mind, through intuition and reasoning, can discover the existence of the living soul. When I first met George, I told him that either he was pathological (and that his entire book was a figment of his imagination), or that he was fantastic (a lay scientist who had successfully integrated love and logic for the highest spiritual purpose). We can now say, with the independent verification by Laurie Campbell, that George is a scientist medium with a message that speaks to all of us.

You are about to embark on a wondrous journey that celebrates life in a living energy universe. May you feel as inspired and blessed by this book as we have.

—Gary E. Schwartz, Ph.D.

Acknowledgments

Ludwig and Annabel Keller, and the Keller family.

Gary Schwartz and Linda Russek, for their love and determination. I owe the publication of this work to their efforts to investigate my claims and stretch the limits of science.

Brian Hurst, who was the first person to encourage me to keep writing, and who "broke the code."

The Scole Experimental Group: Robin and Sandra Foy, Alan and Diana Bennett, for an unforgettable experience.

Judith Guggenheim, my mentor and great friend. Judith and Bill Guggenheim for pioneering research of the study of after-death communications (ADCs).

Joel Rothschild, for his guidance and direction.

Robert Friedman, who believed in bringing this work to press.

Richard Leviton, my editor, for his wisdom and wit.

Mary Anna Walker, who was unconditionally supportive from the beginning, along with Andrea Tutone and Helen Aldine Foley.

Michael Brimhall, whose support and humor are invaluable to me.

I thank my mother, who listened.

Ulla Simic, who shared her extraordinary experiences with a total stranger, and without whom there may have been no book.

Alice Wilson, who made good on our pact.

Mimi Wilson, who helped edit, and made suggestions from the start.

Gary Stella, who also helped edit my early attempts to document my experiences.

Bill Wynn, my best friend, and Gregg Hood, who reminded me that there is no such thing as "too far gone."

Patrice Desvarieux, for his open mind.

Kim Dower, for her perfect pitch.

Lee Roloff, Ph.D., who introduced me to the work of Carl Jung, and taught me how to dream.

Alice Miller, who is my shooting star, and my glee.

Renee Rogers and Steve Witting, who kept me laughing.

Rachel and Katie Sparer, who provided valuable support and feedback.

Nancy and Paul, whom I miss.

Robert Brown, who "knew" I was writing a book before anyone else did.

Thorsten Jacques: thanks for sticking by me from the beginning.

Angelina Usai: thank you for the roses and your skepticism.

Ann Serrano Lopez and Elizabeth Fowler, who supported my going out on a limb.

Richard Gore, who believed in me.

John Leslie Blair, for technological support.

The Milligans, Wilsons, Millers, Egans, Roberts, and Jacks.

For Ian Matthew Dalzell, and Theodore Milligan Marcus.

To my brother, Robert, whose skepticism fueled my determination to complete this project.

Soccorro Santiago, who is a special love to me.

Antoinette Bill and Susan Whittaker, for their feedback and support.

Laurie Campbell, director of Mediumship Research Committee, Human Energy Systems Laboratory, University of Arizona, and possibily the greatest spiritual medium I've met.

For John Dlouhy and Maggie Murphy, for their great love and inspiration.

Special thanks to Barbra.

The following is a true story. Conversations are reconstructions based on memory. Medium consultations are taken from verbatim transcripts of sessions preserved on audio tape. Others are re-creations based on memory. The surnames "Bennett" and "Reicher" are pseudonyms. All other names are those of the actual parties involved.

Dietrich: noun. German for a key to all doors (skeleton key).

Chapter One

Incident

"Based upon our research, we conservatively estimate that at least 50 million Americans, or 20% of the population of the United States, have had one or more after-death communication."

—from *Hello From Heaven!*
by Bill Guggenheim and Judy Guggenheim

Have you ever wondered what it would be like to continue communicating with a loved one after death? My firsthand experiences have demonstrated that such a thing may be possible.

As you will see in the pages that follow, I present evidence of what appears to be a series of contacts between this world and what appears to be a spirit world we call "heaven."

I credit the best-selling author and spiritual medium, James Van Praagh, for opening the door to my experience, and for creating a greater public awareness of the phenomena of mediumship and after-death communications (ADCs). The random act of seeing a television demonstration of mediumship by Van Praagh led me to an unconventional path in which I used mediumship in an experimental way to help a family in bereavement.

It stands to reason that, if the human spirit "survives" physical death, a determined loved one should be able to communicate through a medium. In an informal experiment, I tested mediumship by both acting as a medium and by consulting professional mediums in an attempt to test this hypothesis.

The resulting experiences changed my life and touched the lives of a group of people in a therapeutic way. It is my conviction that our story carries the potential to help redefine spirituality and the way we look at life after death. I hope that publication of this story will help establish and further a need for serious research of ADCs and mediumship.

A graduate of Northwestern University, I achieved a masters in social work from Barry University. I am licensed by the Board of Behavioral Sciences in the State of California (LCS 19150), and am presently employed as a psychiatric social worker by the Los Angeles County Department of Mental Health.

In the course of my work at a community mental health center, I have struggled to help my clients cope with bereavement as well as with major depressions resulting from loss.

As a therapist, I constantly seek to refine the art of intervention and to make a difference in people's lives. That I stumbled onto the unconventional tool of using mediumship to help a grieving family was the result of a quest to intervene in possibly the most effective manner.

If someone had told me just a few years ago that I would be writing a book about using mediumship and ADCs as interventions for bereavement, I would have been extremely skeptical.

Destiny, however, can cause one's direction in life to take remarkable detours.

It all started with the sudden passing of a great friend in a car accident in Frankfurt, Germany, on June 10, 1996. It began with asking for spiritual contact, and it resulted in a miraculous phenomenon that continues at present writing.

I met Michael Keller in January of 1993 by chance in Fort Lauderdale, Florida, where I was finishing my masters in social work.

A clever, brilliant man with a super sense of humor, at twenty-six Michael held the prestigious position of being one of the youngest pursers in Lufthansa's fleet. He was not a flight attendant, but was in charge of the flight crew.

When we met, it was as if higher powers had reunited a pair of long-lost brothers. Destiny appeared to be at work in ways neither of us could understand, but we accepted it without question. We became inseparable companions in mind, body, and spirit.

Michael fit South Florida into his flight schedule almost weekly, making it his "home away from home." Precocious and willful, Michael was filled with self-determination. He was a rebel who would not take "no" for an answer.

Michael would arrive in Fort Lauderdale with surplus champagne and caviar from the first class pantry on his most recent Lufthansa flight. Each visit became a celebration and a reunion. When Michael and I connected, I felt as if nobody else existed, that nobody was funnier, nobody was wiser. He took center stage, and during the time that I knew him, we shared an unconditional bond of love.

On the surface of it, Michael was a guy who had it

all—youth, good looks, parents who loved him unconditionally, a well-paying job, and world travel at his fingertips.

I wished that our time together would never be limited.

Fate, however, intervened to change the form of our
relationship. As a result of the German tourist killings of
1994, Lufthansa's flights to Florida slowed to a trickle, and
Michael arrived one day to state the obvious: Unless one of
us was willing to sacrifice his career for the relationship
and move to a foreign land, we would have to accept that
we could no longer spend as much time together. We
would see one another once every few months as his schedule would allow, and remain friends.

This was a time of crisis and sadness for both of us, but
I wanted Michael to be happy. Not long afterward,
Michael found a companion named Markus Reicher who
eventually moved into Michael's apartment in Frankfurt,
Germany.

I thought that this would seal Michael's fate for the better, though for Michael something was lacking. He seemed
to be on a kind of spiritual quest for an essential ingredient
in life that seemed to elude him. In truth, he was running
out of time from the moment I met him.

Pivotal to this story is my connection with Michael's
parents.

I visited Michael in Germany in the fall of 1993. I met
his parents, Ludwig and Annabel Keller, over coffee and
cake at their home in Kirschfurt, Germany, a picturesque
village just off the River Main. Intelligent and straight to
the point, they seemed a perfect match of pragmatism and
good humor; a loving couple in their early sixties. I had an
immediate good first impression of them. They clearly

adored Michael, the youngest of three sons. Michael was the baby, the golden son.

I had never seen such love between parents and child before in my life. They laughed and radiated love in each other's presence and celebrated Michael's precocious sense of humor. The mutual love affair among the three of them was beyond description. I sat back and watched this loving connection with fascination and intrigue.

It's important to note that the Kellers were no strangers to loss. Both were children living in Germany during World War Two, and were the young victims of the war's senseless ferocity. Annabel lost two brothers in the war, and Ludwig Keller barely escaped death during a bombing at a Red Cross shelter for women and children. Now, they seemed stronger for having survived these stressors.

Michael's parents went out of their way to make me feel welcome, and they seemed strangely drawn to me. They were supportive of the fact that Michael had linked up overseas with someone who seemed to anchor him and provide him with stability in the maelstrom of his maddening, time-changing flights.

We kept in touch over the four years I knew Michael, on Christmas, birthdays, and holidays. I found them to be two of the kindest and most generous people I've ever met. They became like family to me.

I moved to Los Angeles from South Florida in May of 1996. I hadn't spoken with Michael for several months during the move, so I was completely unprepared when I phoned Frankfurt and learned from Markus Reicher that Michael had been killed in a car accident shortly after my move to California.

I immediately phoned Michael's parents, who were in shock. They related that the funeral had already taken place, but that a Requiem Mass would be held for Michael at Laurentius Cathedral in Kirschfurt on July 5, 1996.

I later phoned Michael's brother, Heiko Keller, who explained what had happened. On June 10, 1996 at around 10:00 P.M., on the outskirts of Frankfurt a man stopped to pick up a hitchhiker standing by the side of the road. The hitchhiker was Michael.

He seemed frightened and disoriented. When the driver looked down, he discovered that Michael wasn't wearing any shoes. They drove for a bit, but Michael seemed antsy, and uncomfortable.

Inexplicably, Michael suddenly insisted that the man stop the car so that he could resume walking. The driver argued with him, but Michael was adamant. The driver told him it was dangerous on this stretch of road, there were no streetlights. But Michael wouldn't back down. He got out of the car and closed the door.

The driver was concerned for Michael's safety, and drove to a nearby police station to get help. He insisted the police follow him to where he had left Michael, but when they returned to the site, at 11:10 P.M., it was a horrific scene.

Michael lay dead on the road. One car, a Porsche, had run over him and plowed into a tree. The driver was in critical condition. The other car, a Ford Fiesta, had collided with the Porsche after running over Michael a second time, and the driver was in a state of shock. She had never seen Michael.

No one knew what Michael was doing on that road, how he got there, or why he insisted on getting out of the car that had stopped for him.

The accident scene had been played over and over again in living color, to the Kellers' horror, on Frankfurt's evening news on June 11, and *Die Bild-Zeitung*, Germany's tabloid equivalent of *The National Enquirer*, ran a headline, which read, "Tot-Hitzekoller? (Dead from Heatstroke?)." It featured a gruesome photograph of Michael's body, a trail of blood leading from where he had been hit, as well as photos of the totaled Fiesta and Porsche.

I later discovered that Michael Keller was suffering from depression at the time, and that in the months preceding his death, there were mysterious disappearances and an escalation in his use of stimulants.

Was it just an accident, I wondered, or had Michael played a role in the accident? Was there foul play? There were so many questions left unanswered.

I was devastated by the tragedy of Michael's death, but in the wake of his mysterious passing, a phenomenon was beginning.

Chapter Two

The Rainbow Lights

"I want you to have a view into my soul, something I practically have never afforded to someone else."

—Michael Keller in a letter to me
from February of 1993

June 17, 1996

It was Michael's brother, Heiko Keller, who had the first experience.

He had driven from Laudenbach, Germany, to the roadway outside Frankfurt where Michael had been killed. Drawn by curiosity and a desire to understand how the accident happened, he drove out after the funeral to pay his respects at the site.

The section of highway was actually leading *away* from Frankfurt, and was a good distance from Michael's home or from any known friend or associate. The highway is a narrow road without shoulders. Heiko thought it was certainly not an area where anyone had any business walking.

He pulled his car onto a grassy area adjacent to the site,

and noticed the speed of the cars whizzing past, and how they seemed to come out of nowhere.

At night, Michael wouldn't have had a chance, Heiko thought.

Carefully, he walked along the grassy embankment to the actual place where Michael had lain when the paramedics arrived. He first noticed the hypodermic needles they had used in an effort to resuscitate him. This protocol had been followed even though doctors at the scene could find no pulse in Michael.

Suddenly, as he stared at the site, Heiko saw what appeared to be rainbow-colored lights surrounding the precise spot where Michael's body had lain after the accident. Varying in size and form, the lights danced and darted in front of him, as if in an attempt to communicate with him. To recover his senses, Heiko rubbed his eyes and looked away momentarily at the woods across the street. There was no wind that day, but, strangely, two trees before him began to shake violently back and forth, while the surrounding trees stood absolutely still.

He couldn't believe his senses. He blinked, then turned back to look at the accident scene. The rainbow lights were still there. "Like the fingers of God," he later related to me. Sparkling, and blinking back at him.

Unaware of Heiko's experience, I was on the opposite side of the world, yearning to support Michael's parents in any way I could. I was considering flying to Germany, but wondered how I could make a difference during this terrible crisis.

I had always been skeptical about the existence of life after death. On the other hand, the topic remained a passionate mystery to me for as long as I can remember. I've always believed that, if we survive bodily death, there must be a way to come back and prove to the ones left behind that there is a dimension beyond our present life on Earth.

My quest led me to research the topic of life after death, combing the lists of non-fiction and metaphysical literature for books which provided evidence of life after death. While many authors have explored the subject, only a few publications provided an inkling of what I sought.

I was impressed with the questions raised in *Many Lives, Many Masters* by Brian Weiss, M.D. A Yale-educated psychiatrist, Dr. Weiss put his career on the line by writing about a patient, Catherine, who appeared to have the ability to relay information from another dimension while under hypnosis. In an altered state of consciousness, Catherine talked about life after death, delivering specific information, relevent to Dr. Weiss, from otherworldly "masters," information unknown to Catherine. Furthermore, while under hypnosis, Catherine journeyed through past life experiences and found that her anxiety and depression lessened as a result.

I was intrigued with the phenomenon of near-death experiences (NDEs), which is the focus of *Life After Life* by Raymond Moody, M.D., and *Closer to the Light* by Melvin Morse, M.D. Through current medical advances in resuscitation, Moody and Morse's subjects were brought back from the brink of death; they shared similar postmortem sensations such as floating above their bodies and traveling through a tunnel towards a mystical "light," where they experienced glorious reunions with family members who had "died," but now stood miraculously before them in robes of light.

I came to the conclusion that if NDEs were to be taken as a revelation of the existence of another dimension, then surely this could be somehow proven. Someone could give a sign to someone else after death, or phenomena could be witnessed firsthand which could prove beyond a shadow of a doubt that life after death was a matter of fact, not fiction.

Bill and Judy Guggenheim's work, *Hello From Heaven!*, which includes anecdotes from scores of people who reported after-death communications (ADCs) with the spirits of loved ones, hit home with me. The Guggenheims' research indicates that approximately 20% of Americans have experienced one, or more, after-death communication, compared to the estimated 4% of the population who have experienced NDEs. I was impressed that ADC experiences outnumbered NDE experiences four to one. The Guggenheims advocate that continued research of ADCs is warranted by the sheer numbers of respondents claiming to have made contact with loved ones who have physically "died."

While I was greatly intrigued by all I had read on the subject of life after death, I remained somewhat skeptical. Now, Michael's sudden death left me curious for real answers, and I was led to take an inventory of my own mystical experiences.

My first experience with after-death communication occurred in 1993 and resulted in a supernatural intervention which saved my life.

I had a favorite aunt named Alice Wilson who died from lung cancer in November 1987. I had enormous love for Alice, as she was a woman of great humor and strong character. In fact, during a summer vacation before she died, we made a pact on the shores of Lake Erie at Van

Buren Point, New York, that, if there *was* a life after death, the one who "passed" first would try and find a way to communicate a message from the next dimension as proof of life after death.

It was a whimsical collaboration, but an expression of the great love between us, and it came to haunt me a year later when Alice died. Could she send a message through mediumship, I wondered?

I went to Lily Dale, a Spiritualist community near Van Buren Point, New York, in search of a medium with whom Alice could attempt to make good on her promise. Summer after summer I visited Lily Dale, but regrettably, only one medium appeared to provide a message that seemed authentic, and its portent left me skeptical.

It wasn't until I had met Michael Keller that Alice finally got back to me.

Driving north on I-95 from Miami to Fort Lauderdale, I found myself behind a drunk driver and wondered whether to pull over or risk passing him as he swerved from the right lane into the middle lane ahead of me.

Opting to pass in the far left lane and about to hit the gas, out of nowhere came the voice of my Aunt Alice. "I can't help you win the lottery, but I can keep you from dying in a car accident. Pull over now. You're in danger."

As a therapist, I treat people who suffer from hearing voices, so I was taken aback. What was happening? It was such an overpowering experience that I heeded the voice, unmistakably that of my aunt, for we had always joked about winning the lottery and taking our family on a trip out west. The phrase "I can't help you win the lottery" identified her to me and I responded without questioning.

I pulled into a tiny cul-de-sac off to my left and

watched as the drunk driver suddenly careened into my lane, where *another car* appeared in the next lane from out the blue. The three cars would have collided had it not been for the voice warning me to pull over.

When I got home, I called Alice's daughter, Edith Wilson, to say, "You'll never believe what just happened to me . . ."

It was after that event that I discovered a knack for "giving readings." I would be with friends, family, even strangers, and information would suddenly be conveyed to me. At first, I was reluctant to pass these messages along to people, but after a while, I started disclosing these intuitive thoughts that appeared to originate spontaneously and be therapeutic in nature.

The pivotal event that led to the experience that is the focus of this book happened "by chance" shortly before I heard the news about Michael's death.

I was channel surfing one day when I came across the tail end of a television program titled "The Other Side," which featured a controversial medium who immediately captured my attention.

A couple, Lee and Gerene Erickson, sat opposite an enthusiastic, short man with a moustache who was bringing evidential messages to them from a daughter who had died prematurely young. The medium was James Van Praagh, and the messages he brought appeared specific and bore relevance to the Ericksons to such a degree that I had to wonder if it was true contact with the spirit of their daughter.

James Van Praagh would later achieve national fame as the author of *The New York Times* bestseller, *Talking to Heaven*, but at this time he was an unknown. On this episode of "The Other Side," he related: "Your daughter says, 'Tell them they just repainted my bedroom at home. It's green. They just did it since I left them, and I've been to the room and seen it.'"

The mother began to break down and cry and nod her head in affirmation. "Yes! That's true! No one knows that but us," she said, and jubilantly squeezed her husband's hand. "That's her!"

I flipped on the VCR and stuck in the first tape I could find, recording into the middle of a movie I had taped.

Van Praagh's messages appeared to be relayed at lightning speed, with many a bull's-eye "hit" ultimately convincing the grieving Ericksons that Van Praagh had made contact with their daughter's spirit. There were hits, but there were also misses.

Still, I was transfixed. Because I had treated grieving and bereaved clients as a social worker, something about the parents' reaction to Van Praagh's mediumship struck me as real and genuine.

"We just painted her room last week!" the mother announced triumphantly.

"She says, 'I'm all right! I'm all right!'" Van Praagh assured them, and described the deceased girl's physical appearance, the manner of her passing, the time that she died.

Still I wondered, could this be real? Is this guy really talking to their daughter's spirit? I watched as his subjects began to weep with recognition at the facts Van Praagh brought forth. I was amazed, but remained skeptical.

After Michael's death, I remembered Van Praagh and found myself wondering: could Michael *speak to me* and could mediumship somehow help the Keller family in their bereavement? If Van Praagh or other mediums could talk to strangers who had died, and my aunt could speak to me, why couldn't I speak with Michael?

I made a conscious choice to try my hand at mediumship.

Chapter Three

Contact

"It seems that you get every vibe I send out. You must have these big, big invisible antennas that are able to project my visions into your mind . . ."

—Michael Keller in a letter to me
from March of 1993

June 28, 1996

It started off like any other day.

A week and one day had passed since I phoned Markus Reicher and learned the news of Michael's death, and in Los Angeles on the morning of June 28, 1996, I was having second thoughts about going to Germany.

Friends were concerned about the trip and asked, "What are you going to do there? Couldn't you just as well send some flowers to the church? I mean—fly to Germany? For what?" Somehow I couldn't explain why I was drawn to go back to Frankfurt.

Every night for a week after I spoke with Markus, I trekked up the hill on Vermont Avenue towards Griffith Park, and found refuge in a small garden sanctuary adjacent to a nearby church. I sent up prayers for Michael's soul, and for his parents.

Michael's death was a senseless tragedy. Killed walking down the street? After flying around the planet hundreds of times on Lufthansa?

Early every evening, my vigil continued outside the church. I prayed for justice in this matter. Moreover, I prayed for consolation and peace for Michael's family, for the parents who had loved him unconditionally. I felt that I could help his parents somehow. It seemed like the least I could do. So what if I'm walking into a minefield of pain and confusion, I thought.

It was in the meditation of this moment that a decision finally came. You will have regrets if you don't go, I thought. You will regret it for the rest of your life.

Shortly after returning to my apartment, a courier knocked at the door with the airline ticket to Frankfurt.

At about eleven P.M. that night, exhausted, I lay in bed wondering what I was going to do when I got there. I thought again of James Van Praagh and wondered if it was possible to speak with the spirit of Michael Keller with my mind. Now was the time to find out. Something in me had refused to accept the death, and more to the point, I continued to feel Michael's presence. It was uncanny. It felt as if he was still alive, and close at hand. If only I could communicate with him. Now was the time.

I asked him, "If you're still there, in some spirit world, don't leave your parents in grief. Try and give them a sign that you are O.K. Talk to me." I asked him to give a sign for his partner in Frankfurt, and for Markus Reicher, since I knew he was in shock as well.

What followed was an event that would change my life.

It wasn't what I expected, but neither was it like a face-to-face encounter with a ghost. At times, it was like free-associating, but the responses to questions that I posed were filled with startling details and also seemed to be the whispers of Michael Keller. In the silence of meditation, I asked for some answers.

"Tell me something to tell your father," I asked.

An answer came. "Tell him that they have taken my childhood teddy bear and put it in their bedroom. Sometimes, they sleep with it. It's on or near their bed."

I got out of bed and got a pad and pen and began writing. I was awake, obviously. This was not a dream.

I asked, "Do you have a message for your mother?" He whispered, "I bought her a present this year—a red scarf. Ask my mother, 'Why don't you wear it?'"

He repeated, "Tell her to wear my red scarf. She didn't wear it when I gave it to her."

I asked for a message for his companion: "What can I tell Markus Reicher?"

Another message: "Tell him that we share a jacket, a black leather jacket, and tell him that I want it back. He can't keep it." They shared a jacket? I had never seen a photo of Markus Reicher and had no idea if he was Michael's size.

"I want it returned to my family." Michael was adamant.

Seeking another message, I asked, "What more can I tell your parents?"

He whispered, "Lufthansa will send a check in the mail to my parents for a policy in which they are named as beneficiaries. It will pay off my debts."

Markus isn't the beneficiary, I wondered?

Further, Michael described the accident; he conveyed that it happened not far from the side of the road. He had been partying, and some people had left him on the road; he had been uncomfortable and very thirsty, and had stepped a little bit out into the road, assuming that the driver would stop for him.

"She didn't stop," Michael said. "She wasn't looking at the road." All the time he was *sure* that she would stop, so he didn't move. Suddenly, he said, he found himself looking down over the accident, seeing his body and the wrecked car. "I thought, 'Uh-oh.' I was on the road, and now I was above it looking down!"

"Was it scary?!" I asked. The answer shocked me. He said that he thought the whole thing was "funny." It amused him. He was capable in spirit, he conveyed, of looking down on the whole scene, and enjoyed the pleasure of the autonomy of seeing this scene, and not feeling any pain. It was a new adventure for him. He conveyed that someone was with him after the accident, some "spirit person" to help him along.

I then asked, "Well, how does heaven feel? What's it like?"

His reply: "Warm."

I pressed on: "Can you describe heaven?"

After a moment of silence the reply came, "There is no imitation. You cannot imitate it."

Was I talking to myself? Was this mediumship? How could I tell that it wasn't just free association?

I got what I was looking for, if this was for real: messages of consolation for Michael's family and for Markus Reicher. Bewildered and emotionally drained, I began to fade, and after writing down the messages, I fell into a deep sleep.

The next morning, I didn't know how to react to the messages. I looked at the notes I'd hastily scribbled on my notepad. This experience raised more questions than it answered, but still, I had documented the information with the hope of helping a family grieving an enormous loss. How to relay it, though? These scribbled notes formulated the beginning of what later became an ongoing series of paranormal events related to after-death communication with Michael Keller.

On July 3, 1996, I risked considerable embarrassment by faxing the following information to Michael's brother, Heiko Keller:

"Strange as this may sound, I feel that your brother's spirit has sent these communications through mediumship:

1. Ludwig has taken Michael's childhood teddy bear from Michael's Frankfurt apartment and the bear is in their bedroom in Kirschfurt. He has it on or near his bed.
2. Michael and Markus 'share a jacket,' a black leather jacket, and, for whatever reason, Michael doesn't want Markus to have it.
3. Ludwig and Annabel are named as beneficiaries via Lufthansa in an accidental death insurance policy, and Michael says Lufthansa should be sending them a check in the mail.
4. Michael has recently given a red scarf to Annabel, and it's like a joke between them; will she wear this red scarf?"

Unbeknownst to me, on the same evening of June 28, 1996, halfway around the world in Muhlheim, Germany, a woman I hadn't met named Ulla Simic, a colleague and friend of Michael Keller's, underwent a supernatural experience so strange that she felt compelled to write about it in her diary, since there was no one close at hand she felt comfortable sharing it with.

I would have to fly to Germany to learn the astonishing details of her visual contact with the spirit of Michael Keller.

Chapter Four

Get Here

"You can reach me by railway, you can reach me by Trailway, you can reach me by airplane, you can reach me with your mind."

— from "Get Here" by Brenda Russell

Now I was curious.

My mind told me that it was impossible, but as I sat and stared at the small writing tablet before me, the temptation to seek confirmation of these messages was overwhelming.

I could call Germany—I could find out if there was anything to this. A few overseas calls to Michael's folks and Michael's friends, asking a couple of questions, and I could get to the bottom of this.

Either I had made contact with Michael, or it was a product of my imagination. I had to find out. I worried that I might anger or confuse Michael's parents, but the potential for healing was enormous.

Ethically, it would be inappropriate for me as a clinical social worker to use mediumship in a professional setting since it has rarely been the focus of any serious scientific research. In the context of a personal loss, however, I felt an urge to follow through with passing along the strange messages I'd received.

It took a couple of days to get my courage up, but while taking a break from packing for the Frankfurt trip, I called Ludwig Keller. After expressing condolences over his loss, I sandwiched in a question: "Ludwig, I know this is a strange question, but did Michael have a childhood teddy bear in his apartment in Frankfurt?"

"Yes. It was his Steiff bear," he said.

I was stunned. I had no knowledge that Michael kept a Steiff bear in his apartment in Frankfurt.

Hedging and not knowing how to delve further, I continued, "How old is this Steiff bear?"

"Michael . . . had this bear since he was five years old. It was his favorite. We gave him many Steiff animals, but this one he kept in the apartment."

O.K. A bear. But what about the second part of the message?

"Did you pick the bear up in Frankfurt and take it back to your home in Kirschfurt?"

"Well—yes! We took it on one of the first days after the accident. Annabel told you?" he asked.

I avoided answering this question.

"I'm just curious. And tell me, did you put this bear in your bedroom . . . ?" I winced on the other end of the line.

Ludwig was shocked.

"Yes. Yes! But how do you know this? Annabel told you?"

I was stumped to explain it.

"Well, I . . . I don't know how to say this." I decided to

blurt it out. "Ludwig, I feel that Michael told me this. I don't know how. How else would I know these things?"

"That's true, the first day we went to Michael's apartment on Toengesgasse in Frankfurt, we took a few of his things with us, and the bear came with us then. Who told you the bear was in our bedroom? No one knows that!"

I stalled for time.

"Ludwig, please let me explain more when I come to Germany."

So one of the messages was true after all.

I called Michael's best friend in Germany, Thorsten Jacques, to ask for help in finding a place to stay when I came to Frankfurt. A witty German in his early thirties, Thorsten had been Michael's best friend and neighbor for years, and had lived above him in Michael's building at 46 Toengesgasse. I had met Thorsten during my trip to Frankfurt in September of 1993.

"You know I'm working and can't make it, but I'm sending Markus Reicher to meet you at the airport. We're worried about him; he's taken Michael's death very hard. We worry that he could be suicidal. Perhaps you can help him? I trust he will find you at the airport."

"How will I know him? I've never met him." I said.

"Just go to the bar outside the Continental gate. He'll be the one who looks like he lives there." Markus, it turned out, was an alcoholic.

I took the opportunity to inquire for more details about the mysterious accident that had cost Michael his life.

"Can you explain more about what happened?" I asked.

"Really, the one you should talk with is Michael's colleague, Angelina Usai. She was with Michael the day before he died, and she knows more than I do, unfortunately. I was in Chicago on vacation when all of this happened."

Angelina and I had once spoken by phone while Michael was laid over in Miami, but we had never met in person.

"Very well, then. I'd like to meet Angelina. But, first, Thorsten, I have a question."

I hesitated, then asked about the part of the message regarding Michael's partner, Markus Reicher.

"Yes?" he asked.

"Thorsten, this is a strange question, but was there a black leather jacket that Michael owned that he shared with Markus? I never saw Michael wearing one, but I'm curious."

"Yes. They both fit into this jacket, Markus didn't have many nice things. Michael made considerably more money than Markus, and sometimes Markus would borrow some. Why do you ask?"

"It's not important, Thorsten." Then I switched gears, and came out with it.

"O.K. This is going to sound strange, but I feel like I've been able to communicate with Michael. I prayed for information to console his parents and Markus. I got the message, 'We share a black leather jacket, and *I want it back.*' I thought, 'You can't have it back, you're not alive anymore,' and Michael's response was, 'Markus is *not* to have this jacket.'"

"How strange!" Thorsten replied. "The parents just came to pick up that jacket last week. Markus wanted it, but they've given it to Michael's nephew, Phillip Keller."

That night, I had a dream that I was in Germany. In the twilight, mountainous peaks cast dark blue and violet shadows as I made my way up a hill into a mist. I recognized the terrain surrounding me. It was the sprawling countryside in Kirschfurt, home of the Keller family.

Just as I passed the familiar gate to the Kellers' home, a child of about seven years old greeted me, and I knew somehow he belonged there. He was excited to see me, as if he had been expecting me.

He took my hand, and led me up the hill farther, towards the house. The boy danced in front of me with glee as I strained to place him. He was a Keller for sure, but was it one of Michael's nephews, Phillip or Carston Keller? It was only when we had made it up the hill and approached the front door of the house that I understood that the child was Michael.

On the morning of July 4, 1996, I drove to Los Angeles International Airport and boarded the Continental flight. During our take-off and ascent, I was still thinking about the messages from Michael. Hollywood shrunk to the size of a pea below as we continued to rise higher, eventually breaking through the clouds and sailing into the blue stratosphere. Cruising at 30,000 feet, I was thrust back into Michael's world, the one he loved. Here, in Michael's world, I remembered the day we first met.

It was at The Cathode Ray, a bistro nestled just off Las Olas Boulevard in Fort Lauderdale the first week of January, 1993.

Behind me, a stranger walked up to the bar clutching a small backpack and, chuckling at the TV screen, ordered a martini straight-up with an olive. He took out a pack of Davidoff cigarettes from his navy blue Ralph Lauren jacket and placed them on the bar, raising one carefully to his lips and igniting it with an elegant, sterling silver lighter.

He opened a plaid wallet, paid for the drink, and tipped the bartender one dollar with aplomb, segregating the American dollars from his blue- and red-colored Deutschmarks.

I noticed the bills and, out of curiosity, I asked, "What country are those from?"

"Germany. Michael." He smiled, offered his right hand, and, with his left, dug into his backpack, retrieved a large hardbound book and plopped it down on the bar. "I was just up the block having supper when I just thought I'd check this place out . . . I don't even know why I came in!"

He began to thumb through the volume on the bar.

Curious, I asked, "What are you reading?"

He responded, "It's a biography of Marlene Dietrich by her daughter, Maria Riva." He held up the book, and on the cover was a haunting 1930s photo of Dietrich by Josef Von Sternberg, her eyes staring placidly into eternity. "You know, star of *The Blue Angel!*" He beamed.

As I picked up the book, I asked, "What does her daughter say that fits into a book that big?"

He defended Dietrich: "A lot. I like her, because she does whatever the hell she wants and says exactly what's on her mind. She says the funniest things." Dietrich had died in 1992, but Michael spoke about her in the present tense, like Dietrich was off in Paris, somewhere, or closer still— watching the TV monitor at a table behind us, taking cool puffs from a foot-long cigarette filter. He took a sip of his martini, and began to quote:

"Listen to this: 'Dietrich didn't like God. He could make things happen over which she had no control. This frightened her and made *Him* the enemy.'" Laughing, Michael took a puff from his cigarette and exhaled, aiming the trail at the ceiling and away from the book as if it were the Bible. "And listen to this—so funny. Dietrich said that Greta Garbo was so stingy that she used to count all of the sugar cubes to make sure that her maid had not taken a single one. Unbelievable." He chuckled.

"Wasn't Dietrich an alcoholic, too?" I asked.

"Sure, she partied a little bit." He minimized this aspect, and his epistle continued: "Even though Dietrich didn't like God, she was very superstitious. She was so frightened to fly on airplanes that she would take out a little chamois bag containing a gold chain with all these lucky medallions: a cross, a medal of St. Christopher, a Star of David, a rabbit's foot, even her zodiac sign."

We both laughed. I was charmed.

"So much for God being the enemy!" I pointed out.

Michael explained that he loved Dietrich because she seemed to tower over and conquer reality.

Curious about this uncommon tourist, I asked, "Why have you come here now?"

"I'm a purser for Lufthansa. Fort Lauderdale is one of my bases, and I never get to stay anywhere for very long, so I'm actually here alone on vacation, making up for lost time."

"A flight attendant?" I asked.

He corrected me, stating emphatically, "Pursers *give* the orders, and flight attendants *take* the orders." He watched my expression, paused, took a sip of his martini, and lit another Davidoff.

"It's hard work, actually. I mean, sometimes people can be so dumb. My last trip, someone from the ground crew tried to load the meals before they were due, and he wheeled the tray onto the deck, and I said, 'This doesn't

28

come on just now.' He argued with me, and then I wheeled him and his cart right off the plane and back into the terminal."

I laughed.

While Michael minimized the demands of his job, the responsibility for the flight crew and passengers of each flight was enormous. Already, he had several years of international flights under his belt.

"Where do you fly?" I asked.

"Paris, London, the Maldives, Gibraltar, Lisbon, Bangkok, Mauritius, United Arab Emirates, Tokyo, Sydney, Australia, Dakar, Africa, Havana, the Bahamas, Cancun, the Dominican Republic, Puerto Rico, New York, and . . . what's left?

Mars?"

I couldn't believe a person so young had been to so many places.

"I've seen the world from first class and there's only one drawback—time changes. One morning I flew from Frankfurt to the Seychelles Islands, and the sun never set, I turned around and flew back to Frankfurt—still daylight, now 12 hours or something. I landed, then flew to Montego Bay, Jamaica, dead-head [as a non-working passenger], after having slept maybe an hour on the plane from Germany, only to arrive, check into the hotel, shower, take a nap, and turn around to fly as a crew member to Fort Lauderdale."

"How do you do it?" I asked. "I couldn't work like that. I couldn't function on that level of exhaustion."

"My little friends." He reached into his backpack, and pulled out a pack of No-Doz, popped one out of its case, and took it as if it were a vitamin.

"That's not a very healthy remedy for jet lag." I observed with caution.

"Do you want me to fall asleep while I'm talking to you?" He made a joke of it.

"I don't like to stay any place for too long. I get—how do you say it? Antsy? Even in Frankfurt, which is where I am from. I get antsy if I'm there for more than a few days. In a week, I can barely stand it. What do you do?"

"I'm a therapist." I responded.

"Great! Free therapy during my vacation!" he added humorously and raised a toast.

So began a challenging long-distance relationship.

Now, halfway across the Atlantic, I was haunted by the way Michael had badly needed support and stability, and how his choice of work undermined his struggle. Adventuresome as he portrayed his job to be, it was draining him of life force, and he fought the time changes at first with caffeine, and then moved on to a stronger remedy—cocaine.

I recalled the strange last words he said that night as we bid each other farewell for the first time: "Protect me from this world."

Chapter Five

Frankfurt

"Let's insist on miracles!"

—Michael Keller
in a postcard to me from June, 1993

July 5, 1996

As the crescent sun peeked sliver-like over the edge of the German horizon and we began our descent, I remained unaware that a metaphysical drama was about to unfold.

Frankfurt is a center of international commerce, the banking capital of Germany and Europe. Frankfurt is also a connecting stop for most European travelers, a place between destinations. For Michael Keller, the airport had been a home of sorts, a vital intersection between departures and arrivals. When the jet pulled up to Continental's gate at the terminal, I peered out the window to discover that we were surrounded by dozens of Lufthansa planes. Now far away, Los Angeles seemed like another world in another universe.

The Frankfurt airport is as quiet as a library, and as I passed through customs, I felt struck again with a sense of urgency that there was a message to deliver to Mrs. Keller. I wondered if I had the courage to follow through with it. I was also deeply curious for information as to why Michael's life had been cut short, and eager to be supportive to Michael's friends and parents.

I approached the bar outside the gate where Markus Reicher sat waiting. He was a tall man in his twenties with blond hair and blue eyes, yet I had to imagine his non-grieving countenance, because his face was lined and creased from stress, and his eyes were bloodshot. When I walked up to him, he burst into tears. It was clear that the sorrow we shared was the same one, and we cried together.

Markus is not fluent in English, and it was obvious that he had already fortified himself with several drinks before my arrival. Overcome with emotion, he tried to explain that he had been powerless to prevent this tragedy. The last few months with Michael were like a roller coaster of confusion as Michael crumpled due to the demands of his work schedule coupled with his use of stimulants. Now he was gone, and Markus was alone.

Markus struggled to explain some of the facts in broken English as we boarded the U-Bahn to make our way to Frankfurt. I could see that broaching the subject of the messages was beyond the reach of the language barrier between us, so I focused on talking about the present situation until we reached downtown Frankfurt, and we made our way to Michael's building at 46 Toengesgasse.

I walked into Michael's apartment. It looked undisturbed from my visit in 1993. It was also strangely without a feeling of loss. I had the sensation that he had just stepped out, and was keeping us waiting, that he was not really dead.

Markus left the apartment to go across the street to a restaurant for a bite to eat and another cocktail, leaving me alone to unpack and shower for the mass. I was alone in the apartment for a minute when Michael's telephone rang.

"George?" a woman's voice asked with unexpected urgency.

"Yes?" I answered.

"I'm a colleague of Michael's. I fly for Lufthansa. I just wanted to call you to say I think it's great that you flew all the way to go to this mass. You are a true friend." The voice was young, vivacious.

"Is this Ina?" I asked. Michael had told me about a best friend and fellow Lufthansa crewmember named Ina Tharandt, and I expected to hear from her. His death had to be a shock to her.

"No, this is Ulla. Ulla Simic. I've been flying recently with Michael," she said.

"Oh, really? Are you going to this mass for Michael?" I asked.

"Well, you see, I'm going with you. I called Thorsten and Markus and told them that I wanted to go to this service. I *had* to, I mean . . ." She cut herself off abruptly, sighed, and took a deep breath. "I just have to say it. I have to see you. I had something very strange happen to me, and I don't, can't, talk about it on the phone. It's about Michael. Something strange." She trailed off.

I was taken aback, and in a hurry to get ready for the trip to Kirschfurt. "Do you mind if we talk on the way then?" I asked.

"Of course not!" she said, and laughed. "Michael told us so much about you—I feel like I know you already."

"I guess we'll pick you up on the way, and you can judge for yourself," I said.

"Bye."

Strange call, I thought. I stepped into Michael's bathroom to take a shower, and welcomed the hot stream of water on my face and hair as I became acclimated to being on the other side of the world. I turned to look out the window and noticed that something had been added since my last visit. Staring back at me from the ledge lay a recent purchase of Michael's: a small statue of a cherub, smiling, its wings aloft and its hands lifting to the heavens.

When I came out of the shower, there was a knock at the door. I opened it, and Thorsten Jacques extended his hand.

"George, welcome back to Germany," Thorsten was solemn.

"Thorsten, can you fill me in?" I asked. "How did this happen?"

Thorsten walked in and continued speaking. "It's unbelievable. In a way, I know, and in a way, I don't know. Michael just seemed to go crazy these last two months; he was so depressed, and yet always going out to party, night after night, disappearing all the time. I hardly saw him, because he would sleep through the day, and be up all night, flying off on a broomstick here, there. He started missing flights. At first, he would call in sick, and then, finally, he wouldn't answer the phone—he would be on stand-by, and he wouldn't answer the phone."

"I can't believe this," I said. "I didn't see any of this when I saw him just two months ago."

Thorsten continued, "'They've taken control of my life!' he told me right before I left for Chicago. He was speaking of the airline. 'I don't have a moment's peace.' Well, everything had become so *extreme* for him. It all took its toll. Lufthansa knew something was wrong. They sent him to see a shrink, Dr. Roland Kulhanek, and that's where he went the day he died, to Dr. Kulhanek's office at Lufthansa's administration building."

"Michael saw a psychologist?" I asked.

"The day he died," Thorsten added, indicating the irony of it.

"The family says that Dr. Kulhanek told him, 'No problem. We'll work with you, we'll help you straighten out your schedule, and if you have a drug problem, we'll provide treatment.' They were totally understanding. He left the building, and someone saw him drive off in someone else's car, not his own Cabriolet. His car is missing."

"They don't know where his car is?" I asked.

"It's a mystery—this whole thing is a mystery, I can tell you!" Thorsten stood before the living room mirror and looked at himself as if he didn't quite register his own image.

"The parents are heartbroken. I don't know what to say! What do you say to them—their boy gets killed at 29 years old, in such a way, and no one knows why? What do you say?"

"Thorsten, what do you think about the messages, and what we discussed—the shared leather jacket the family took from Markus?"

"So strange. Markus was always borrowing Michael's things." Suddenly, his tone changed dramatically as his confession continued. "Now, I tell you this, and don't think too much on it!" Thorsten cautioned me as he straightened his tie in the mirror. "After I heard the news, the first thing I did was to call a Catholic friend of mine—mind you, I'm not religious, but I had to call. I asked her, 'What is the ritual that you do when someone dies to make sure that they don't appear to you?'"

"What?" I was stunned.

"The ritual so the spirit doesn't appear to you. I had the funny feeling that Michael's spirit would appear to me."

This was strange. I was familiar with most phobias, but I had never heard of one like that. "Do you believe in life after death?"

"No, but I wanted to do this ritual *just in case*." Thorsten was funny.

"Well, it's not exorcism?" I asked. "Exorcism takes place when a spirit goes into you and won't leave. You want to make sure that Michael's spirit doesn't even show up. Is there such a ritual in Catholicism?" I was genuinely curious now that he had brought it up.

"This friend said there is no ritual for that, but that I should just go to Liebfrauenkirche, the church on Toengesgasse where they had Michael's funeral, and go to the back part of the sanctuary and light a candle and say a prayer."

"What gave you the idea that Michael would appear to you after he died?" I was curious.

"I don't know! I can't explain it, and don't bring it up again, I tell you."

"Why are you telling me this now?" I asked.

"I don't know. I just wanted to let you know that you're not crazy. I had the same feeling like something was going to happen, that's all."

With a final tug, Thorsten straightened his tie. We left the apartment, descending the dark staircase and crossing the street to find Markus Reicher sitting alone at the restaurant, staring into space, nursing a beer. I noticed several empty shot glasses close by, not pushed far enough away from him for me to miss the fact he was fortifying himself for the trip to Kirschfurt. He was killing the pain in the only way he knew how.

We walked down the street, bought some flowers to take to the cemetery, rented a car at a local vendor, and took off to pick up Ulla. We were off to say goodbye to Michael.

Or so we thought. . . .

Chapter Six

Ulla

"You do not run into such a soul mate every day, perhaps only one or two more in a lifetime."

—from *Only Love Is Real*
by Brian Weiss, M.D.

While we approached the heart of the city of Muhlheim, a light rain began to fall. The cobblestone streets became narrower and the buildings seemed to grow larger and lean out over the road. Cars came within inches of broadsiding us as we barreled down Hausener Strasse to Ulla's modest, two-story apartment complex. I wondered what mysterious revelation led her to call me. Why had she insisted on meeting me now?

"It's a wonder *we* haven't had an accident." I noted as the cars whizzed past us.

Thorsten informed me, "We have to stop at the Kellers on the way to the mass. And by the way, this is *not* America. This is Germany. People have a destination when they drive here and are not merely showing off their BMWs and Mercedes."

This was Thorsten's special sense of humor. Never minding the outcome of two world wars, Thorsten loved to point out Germany's technological superiority over other nations.

He was right, though. The clock was ticking, and it would be embarrassing to arrive late for the mass. Markus, woozy from his cocktails, verged on dozing off in the front seat as we reached Ulla's building. Parking hurriedly, Thorsten pulled the hand brake up and I opened the passenger door and raced up to ring Ulla's buzzer.

Ulla Simic descended the stairs behind the glass security door and stopped for a moment when she saw me. She was brunette, dressed conservatively in a gray wool suit. Her blue eyes searched me out with a kind of little-girl stare. She seemed to recognize me. A beautiful girl, I thought. Extremely attractive. I stood in the rain while she exited the building and opened her umbrella.

"Ulla?" I held the door for her.

"We should go—George?" she put her arm around me cautiously as we crowded into the back seat.

Thorsten then sped off toward the Kellers' home.

Ulla moved close to me and became at once intimate. "It's crazy, but—I had to see you, I don't know why!"

Finally, I had time to vent my feelings about the situation. "This whole thing is crazy. Michael flies around the world hundreds of times, and gets run over walking down the street!"

"We just had a flight in the last two months! We went to the Dominican Republic. Me, Michael, and another girl-friend of his, Angelina Usai. I wouldn't have dreamed all of this could happen. There was nothing so out of the ordinary . . . except."

"Yes?"

"Nothing. He seemed fine. I knew that he partied sometimes, but nothing explains this!" she added.

"I agree. No one has been able to explain this to me, how this happened, what he was doing hitchhiking. That was totally unlike him," I added.

"But I had to see you as soon as possible. I have to tell you the strangest thing that happened a week ago. You're not going to believe this. I was standing in my bathroom putting on my make-up before a flight, when I suddenly heard this sound, like I felt that there must be hundreds of bees."

"Bees?"

"Yes! You heard right, bees, in my ear. Like a buzzing, BZZZZZZZ! Then I turned to look, and *it was Michael*! It was his spirit, but it was like—it appeared to me to be like a tube, a tube of electric energy in the middle of the air! Through this circling tube, I saw his image—plain as day."

As Ulla related this story her blue eyes were glued to mine without distraction. Her sincerity was obvious.

"Ulla—were drugs or alcohol involved in any way?" I asked.

"No! I hadn't taken anything. I don't use drugs, and I rarely drink." She was adamant.

"Are you really saying that Michael appeared to you as a spirit after he died, and you were fully awake when this happened?" I asked, incredulous that someone else was sharing this weird experience.

"That is exactly what I'm saying—there is no doubt at all that this was Michael. I recognized him. He stayed for less than a minute, then he disappeared. I was so frightened, I felt like this energy would go right through me, but it didn't, thank God!"

"So it was scary?"

"I was so frightened that I almost called and canceled my flight! I was to fly on a European trip. I almost missed my flight." She brushed her bangs, and glared at me. "Do you believe me? This was not my imagination. I am certain of that."

"Yes. I certainly do. But I have to ask you why you're telling me this?" I asked.

Ulla looked, became slightly teary eyed, and looked me right in the eye.

"I don't know. I honestly don't." She shrugged her shoulders and blinked.

Ulla was unaware of the fact that the experience she was describing appeared to be a textbook example of the Guggenheims' definition of an ADC: "An after-death communication is a spiritual experience that occurs when someone is contacted directly and spontaneously by a deceased family member or friend."

"Ulla, what day did this happen?"

"I wrote it down in my diary, but I remember. It was last Friday, June 28."

Hearing this, I nearly leaped through my skin. I felt Michael's urgency creeping into the situation all at once, a compelling reminder and another message. In his absence, I felt his presence.

"Yes, I believe you. I do." I tapped Thorsten on the shoulder and asked, "Are you listening to this?"

He pulled his shoulder away from me.

"Don't touch me while I'm driving. It is raining, and any minute now we'll run off the road. Talk to me after we get there, please." The conversation in the backseat was giving him the willies.

41

"Just keep listening, will you?" I asked. I turned back to Ulla, her eyes still focused intently on me.

I reassured her. "You are not alone, Ulla. I have something to tell you. You won't believe this. On the same day that you had this experience, June 28, I was lying in bed, meditating, and I heard what sounded like Michael's voice."

I told her about the four messages, and the conversation with Ludwig.

"Heiko is going to clarify the remaining messages after the mass."

"I'm frightened!" Ulla cried out.

I attempted to reassure her.

"Ulla, something incredible has happened. What are the odds that two strangers would have these experiences with Michael on opposite ends of the world on the same day?" I reached out and held her hand.

"Something's happening . . ." Ulla observed, and took a deep breath as she leaned against me. The clouds let loose a torrent of rain.

Thorsten spoke not a word as Markus began to snore. He had passed out.

Chapter Seven

Resurrection

"Just remember, and don't lose sight that those who are supposed to get the message . . . will!"

—John Edward, in a note to author, May 2001

As we approached the mountainous terrain of Kirschfurt, the rain stopped suddenly. We pulled up to the Keller estate at 12:50 P.M., leaving ten minutes to drive to Laurentius Cathedral for Michael's Requiem Mass. Michael's mother, Annabel Keller, waited for us on the front steps.

An attractive, stylish woman in her early sixties, her beauty at first disguised the fact that she was in enormous pain. I noticed she wore a black scarf. I could hear Michael's voice insisting: "Tell her to wear the red scarf, the red one." We spoke no words, only hugged. Behind her stood Ludwig, Michael's father. He was like a heartbroken statue; absent from his face were all traces of humor and grace that I'd become accustomed to from our first meeting. We shook hands, then I leaned over to hug him. I didn't know what to say. My experience in crisis intervention was of little help in this atmosphere of heartbreak. This isn't happening, I thought to myself. It's not real. "I'm so sorry," I said. And yet I had come to find out something.

After we arrived at Laurentius Cathedral, I took Ulla by the hand, and joined Thorsten and Markus in a pew behind the Kellers.

The service, performed in German, lasted less than an hour. The priest seemed especially caring with the Keller family, directing the service to the front rows where Ludwig and Annabel congregated with Michael's brothers, Ralph and Heiko, and Michael's nephews. I sat quietly with Ulla who translated important points in the sermon.

As the service concluded, I stepped outside with Ulla, Thorsten, and Markus, and approached Heiko.

"George?" he asked, seeing that I was the only person there that he didn't know.

"Heiko?" I asked, noting his uncanny resemblance to Michael.

"First off, thank you for coming. It means a lot that you would make this trip, and the family considers you a true friend. We're very grateful." Heiko's manners and tone were ambassador-like, friendly and courteous.

"I felt protective of Michael in life, Heiko. I had to come. Has anyone come forward to explain what happened, or why this happened?"

"No. One woman is in the hospital and may die as a result of the accident. She's unconscious, and the other driver says she didn't see him. She's in shock. So, no one really knows. One family is asking our family for damages because there were drugs in Michael's system, and they blame him for the accident, for hitchhiking and thus causing the accident."

"They hit him in the accident, and they want to sue your parents?" I was incredulous.

"That's the way the law works in Germany." Heiko said resignedly.

"Do the police suspect foul play?" I asked.

"There will be no investigation. They don't believe anyone else was directly involved, or that it was a homicide."

"You got my fax?" I asked.

"Yes. Your fax is correct about the insurance. There is a policy, and Lufthansa is supposed to pay out after an investigation. My parents are the beneficiaries."

My heart started palpitating. I hedged, then the words came tumbling out.

"Heiko, did you have a chance to ask about the red scarf."

"It's true. Just a few months ago, Michael gave my mother a beautiful red scarf—it's like a Versace, bright red. She showed it to me. And my mother says Michael insisted that she put the thing on the day he bought it for her. It's all true, but I have to tell you, I don't know how you could know these things."

I found myself suddenly crying and turning away from Heiko. It was unlikely that "chance" could account for the accuracy of the messages.

There could be no doubt about it, I thought, as I propped myself up against the church wall. Michael *had* spoken to me that night. It wasn't some kind of delusion, and it wasn't wishful thinking. Apparently, his spirit had survived physical death. Somehow—I didn't know how— Michael had spoken to me from beyond the grave.

Heiko continued, "Now I have something of my own

to tell you . . . ," and he went on to explain how after the funeral he had gone to the place where the accident happened, and seen the strange rainbow-colored lights appear and dance over the place where Michael died. He spoke in hushed tones about the trees that shook with tremendous force when there was no wind.

I became exuberant. Three people—Heiko, Ulla, myself—had shared ADC experiences without prior knowledge that other parties were having similar experiences.

When Heiko finished, I led Ulla by the hand away from the group to the side of the church. "All four of the messages are correct, I said. "The information I got from Michael appears to be on target."

Ulla wiped the tears from my eyes. "Unbelievable." Ulla was bewildered. "He's done this. He brought me here to meet you. I can't explain why I had to seek you out, but this is it—to tell you about my experience, and now, this!"

Suddenly, we were bound together by fate, and I hung close to her.

Michael was buried in a tiny cemetery. There were probably less than fifty people buried there, mostly local citizens of Kirschfurt, and the surrounding areas. Thorsten, Markus, Ulla, and I drove the short way from Laurentius to the grave site, and parked the car.

In the middle of winding, dirt paths leading to the center, a floral tribute befitting a head of state rose up before us like a ripe garden. I held Ulla's hand as we approached the mound of earth and flowers that marked where Michael lay. It was too early for there to be a headstone so a wooden cross tied with a black ribbon served as a temporary marker.

The four of us stood together in silence. Markus wept, still ruminating on what he could have done to prevent Michael's death. Ulla and I looked at each other, and smiled. We whispered our discovery in unison: "He's not there."

When we arrived at the Keller estate for coffee and cake, Ludwig and Annabel welcomed our company and the distraction it provided.

The house was in black. Black ribbons, black bows. A portrait of Michael with a Lufthansa jet in the background stood in a black frame in the center of the living room.

I worked to dispel the depression of the occasion, and found the courage to break the silence. "Michael told me about the Christmas with *Knecht Uberecht*." I ventured.

Annabel started laughing. "Ja, you mean when he was a little boy?" she asked as she balanced a cup of coffee in her hands.

"He told me that when he was seven years old, you both hired someone to play Santa, the *Krist Kind* (Christ child), and that *Knecht Uberecht* is the German Santa Claus who brings a list of all the bad things you've done."

Ludwig chuckled at this.

"He told me that when the actor you hired to play *Knecht* walked through the doorway, Michael came after him with a baseball bat and hit him! Like, how dare you keep score! Don't you open your big mouth and spoil my Christmas!"

Annabel added, "He had the best childhood. No one had that much love."

This was no exaggeration. Though the evidence of that love included material goods, they were mere indications of a love that transcended words.

I asked, "Is Michael's bear here?"

"Yes, yes, it's right over there," Ludwig pointed to the middle of the living room.

Sitting on a chair was the Steiff bear. I approached it like it was an artifact from a Ripley's "Believe It or Not" story, for its link with the first message from Michael haunted me.

"But I thought it was in the bedroom?" Was part of the message wrong?

"It *was*. It was in the bedroom, but we brought it out because we knew you were coming. This is the first day that it is out of the bedroom." Ludwig and Annabel looked lovingly at the Steiff while Thorsten observed the scene with caution and wonder. Ulla smiled.

I stared at the bear for a moment. The Steiff Company has been producing stuffed animals since the early 20th century, and Steiff animals are expensive and very collectible. This Steiff, I thought, was worth its weight in gold. The moment I picked the bear up, it let loose a prolonged growl. Surprised, I nearly dropped it on the floor.

"What was that?" I called out.

The room cracked up with laughter from Thorsten, Ludwig, Annabel, Markus, and Ulla. "Oh, it does that." Ludwig answered, amused at my reaction.

I stood holding the Steiff, now evidence to me that a miracle had taken place. I felt Michael close by, and could sense his satisfaction, almost gloating, that his messages had been delivered. *I told you so.*

I ran my fingers through the bear's fur and watched as the light sparkled and reflected from the bear's sparkling blue eyes. They seemed to blink back at me. I didn't realize it at the time, but my perspective on reality had shifted irrevocably.

Chapter Eight

The Disappearance at Liebfrauenberg

"Eventually we became convinced that some physical phenomena are authentic after-death contacts."

—from *Hello From Heaven!*
by Bill Guggenheim and Judy Guggenheim

July 6, 1996—46 Toengesgasse, Frankfurt

Every week since the accident, Annabel, Ludwig, and Heiko made a pilgrimage from Kirschfurt to Michael's apartment to collect more of his possessions for a last trip home.

Today, they had come to collect some of Michael's books, and empty out a chest of drawers in the hallway. The last thing to go into one bag was a coffee-table book on Marlene Dietrich that I had given Michael in Florida shortly after we met, *Marlene Dietrich: A Hollywood Portrait.*

Upstairs at Thorsten's, there was a knock on the door. Markus entered, and summoned me to go downstairs in his broken English. "The family wants you to go down. Now, please."

Markus walked past me in the direction of Thorsten's kitchen, and opened a bottle of red wine. The Kellers had asked him to leave the apartment during the removal of Michael's things.

The situation was awkward. The Kellers resented Markus for not having intervened to help Michael, and Markus appeared to resent how graciously they welcomed me back into the picture.

Silently, I descended the stairs, knowing that I was walking into the most painful situation I would encounter during this strange visit to Germany.

As I entered the apartment, I could sense the tension in the room, and suddenly I was in the eye of the tornado of emotion created by the accident. A nightmare.

The family called me into the living room, and we all sat and had a good cry. I sat next to Ludwig and put my arm around him, since he and Heiko had taken on the responsibility of keeping Annabel in one piece.

Here and now, the tragedy was felt.

We sat for a short while in silence. Suddenly, Annabel called out for her son:

"Michael! Michael!" She could contain her grief no longer.

Seeing Annabel cry, I felt compelled to console her, but how? I turned my attention to the red scarf; did she understand the meaning behind the message? "Annabel—the red *tuch* . . ." I started.

At this, Heiko suddenly became very agitated; "Please, don't talk about this now!" he piped up. This was no time for supernatural messages from beyond the grave.

Annabel interrupted, "What? What makes you so angry? Go on, George. I want to know!"

At least the crying had stopped. Taking a risk, I pressed on, "Has Heiko explained why I wanted to know about the red scarf Michael gave you a few months ago?"

"No. Heiko hasn't explained anything. Please *you* tell! What is this you want me to know?" Annabel asked.

Due to join Thorsten, Markus, and Ulla at Liebfrauen-berg, an outdoor café just down the block, Annabel insisted, "I'm not going anywhere until someone explains this to me! Please tell me what is so important about this red scarf?"

It was obvious that Heiko had inquired about it, but had withheld the origin behind the message. I looked to Heiko to see how to proceed. He shrugged. A big silence followed.

I explained to Annabel that it seemed that Michael had told *me* that I must tell his mother that he had bought this red scarf recently as a present, and ask her, "Why don't you wear it?"

Annabel nodded, "Yes, he bought me a red scarf. He did want me to wear it. He bought it for me just months ago. He told me to wear it. He bought me a lot of things."

"Yes," I said, "but he told me this two weeks after he died."

"You mean . . . ?" Annabel queried.

The room fell quiet as I observed Annabel's expression, an awareness that conveyed understanding and interest. The walls seemed to smile for a moment.

Walking together in a kind of a spell, we arrived at Liebfrauenberg, joining Ulla, Thorsten, and Markus. I greeted Ulla with a kiss, and we sat together at a table beneath a white umbrella as a waiter approached us to take our order for cocktails.

Ulla leaned over to whisper, "I'm so glad to see you before you go back to the States. I want to keep in touch." I noticed her nervous disposition, and the silver earrings that shook slightly as she spoke.

"We will keep in touch," I assured her.

Breaking the ice, I asked Thorsten to translate anything that might be confusing or complicated for the Kellers.

I told them, "I have something I have to explain: this is the *second* time in my life that I've felt that I've spoken with someone I loved who has died, so this has happened to me once before. I had a favorite aunt and we made a pact that if one of us died, the other one would try to communicate from heaven, if such a thing was possible."

A single bell tolled marking the hour at the Liebfrauenkirche across the way, the church where Michael's funeral had been held less than three weeks before.

I then related the story of how hearing the voice of my aunt had spared me from being in a potentially fatal car accident. Markus shook his head in disbelief and glued his lips to his drink. Ulla appeared to listen more intently as I concluded the story of my first encounter with mediumship.

Thorsten asked, "What do you mean? Did you actually hear a voice out loud?"

I explained, "No, it was more like a spoken thought, but it happened in such a way that I knew it was Alice, my aunt."

Annabel's face lit up with a look of recognition. "Did you know that Michael said his aunt saved *his* life?" she asked.

A look of sudden recognition flashed on Ludwig's face.

Annabel continued: "Michael was in the Dominican Republic a few years ago. He was outside of a casino and watched a taxi pull up to the entrance. A woman he recognized got out of the taxi and entered the casino."

She leaned closer to me, telling her story with great excitement. "He told me that the woman looked *exactly* like my sister, Blondina, who died over five years ago. He used to stay with her in San Francisco on vacations and loved her very much. He was so sure this was my sister that he followed her into the casino. He asked people inside if they'd seen the woman with white hair who had just walked in. No one had seen this woman."

Markus focused his attention away from the table while the rest listened intently.

Annabel's tone intensified. "So, Michael rushed around, trying to find this woman. When he couldn't find her, he returned to the street entrance of the casino to see if she was there. When he got outside, he saw people rushing to the place where he'd been standing across the street. There had been a shooting."

Ulla's eyes became as wide as saucers.

"A man lay bleeding on the street. Michael saw the woman's taxi, and approached the driver. He told Michael that he hadn't dropped off any one, and that he had been sitting there waiting for people to leave. No white-haired woman had come from or gone into this casino."

Ulla began blinking, and her agitation grew as she brought her hands to her ears.

Annabel finished, "Michael said that if he hadn't gone into the casino to look for this woman who looked like my sister, he may have been shot."

At this, Ulla stood bolt upright from her chair, pleading

to those around her, "My God! My earring! Where is it? It was on just a moment ago!"

Thorsten agreed, "I saw you wearing it. Mustn't worry. I saw you wearing two earrings. I'll help you look."

"One must have fallen off," I added.

I now noticed that she was wearing only one silver earring.

Frantic, Ulla cried, "I know I had two earrings! Where is the other earring?!"

Heiko stood up and walked over to her and said, "I'm sure you've just misplaced it, or it slid off or something. It's got to be here."

Nearly hysterical, Ulla searched her purse with her right hand and looked at the ground around her while Heiko crouched and looked below her chair.

A moment later, Ulla panicked and exclaimed, "He's taken my earring! Michael is here and . . . it's gone!"

The Kellers looked on helplessly as the search continued for the missing earring at Liebfrauenberg, while I silently wondered if this was a message from Michael for the six of us.

Chapter Nine

Strange Silhouettes at Toengesgasse

"All psychic and spiritual phenomena are the direct result of the subtle energy interactions between the physical dimension and its parallel energy counterpart."

—from *Adventures Beyond the Body*
by William Buhlman

Ulla did not find her earring. It had apparently vanished from her right ear without a trace.

After the commotion settled at our table, Ulla took the remaining earring off, a temporary solution to a bizarre development. We finished our drinks while reminiscing about Michael, though Ulla remained silent and agitated. She clutched her purse close to her breast as if to prevent mysterious, unseen hands from abducting it.

I thought to myself, it's easy to discount one person's story, one person's strange experience, but now we had all experienced the disappearance of Ulla's earring.

The Kellers, Thorsten, and Markus remained seated at Liebfrauenberg as I took Ulla by the hand and walked silently through the cobblestone alleyway leading to the parking lot.

I asked about what had just happened, and she seemed relieved to reflect on it.

"It just disappeared!" she almost whimpered. "Don't you believe me?"

"I believe you." I reassured her. "You're saying that you think that Michael Keller took your earring."

"Yes! I don't think, I *know* he took it! Heiko and I spread the purse on the ground and looked through everything . . . it's not there! Everyone saw it. . . . Why is he doing this to me?" She implored. Ulla was frightened. If Michael could spirit away some physical object in front of a group of people, what next?

For Ulla, this was a crisis. I realized I had come up with something rational, but I had to be honest with her. I put her feelings into words: "You're afraid that if he can do this, you won't be able to control what he might do next."

"Exactly!" She seemed relieved. "What if I'm driving, and he does something with the light? If he changes it from red to green? Or if I'm on a plane . . . ."

I interrupted: "Why do you think that Michael would do something destructive like that?"

I tried to distract her with an anecdote Michael told me. "Michael loved to play practical jokes. He told me he was expelled from three schools before graduating from high school. One time he told me the funniest story. He had a Latin teacher who kept making fun of him in class. He'd walk over and bop Michael on the head with the Caesar's Latin textbook and tease him for skipping through the hallways, and Michael was determined to get even. He told me that the teacher had a prosthetic leg and that he would routinely take the fake leg off when he went to the bathroom. One day, Michael followed him into the next stall, stole the fake leg, stranding him, and hung the leg on a hook in the hallway with a sign next to it reading, 'Fuck Caesar!' Let's face it. Michael was like a little kid who refused to grow up."

"Unbelievable story." Ulla rolled her eyes.

"Ludwig and Annabel seem to understand about the messages from June 28. They know about your experience, and they know about Heiko's. They understand, and I wouldn't be surprised if Michael snatched your earring in order to make the point that he *is* somewhere, alive and well, and the point is that we're all to accept that fact."

I touched Ulla's cheeks and locked eyes with her.

Ulla hesitated, "Mmm. Yes. I guess—yes. That must be it. He may be trying to send a message with the earring to his parents. That makes sense."

"Good!" I was relieved. "Our situation is unique, Ulla. I find it hard to believe it myself. But the earring—perhaps it proves to his parents that we're telling the truth." I paused. "Take heart, Ulla—probably this is the end of all of this."

Suddenly confident, Ulla straightened herself up, brushed her bangs back with one hand, wiped her eyes and smiled. "Actually, George, I think this is only the beginning."

While Thorsten escorted Markus across the street to Michael's apartment, I walked the Kellers to their Mercedes.

I gathered the courage to sum up our experience. "I believe that your son is safe. I hope you understand what I've tried to say, the messages, and the things Ulla and Heiko have experienced. I will call you when I get back to the United States."

"Thank you for coming all the way from America to say goodbye to our Michael. You are a true friend. I say thank you very much." Annabel paused, tearing up a bit. "You meant so much to Michael. In fact, he just told us the day before he died, 'I want to go to L.A. to see George.' Three weeks ago. I can't believe it."

"Annabel—I think he may have made it to L.A."

"And he said, 'I want to take all of Markus's things and throw them down the stairs!'"

Evidently, more had gone on than I was aware of.

"We miss him," she replied.

"We miss him." Ludwig echoed.

"I'll call you when I get home," I said, hugging them both. "You know, I believe Michael wants you to have this money from the insurance policy. He didn't want to leave you with any debts."

Ludwig paused, then said, "We don't want the money. We want our boy back."

"Maybe he will try to send more messages—somehow." I didn't know what else to say, and I had no clue if the ADCs would continue. I only knew that something compelled me to have faith that it was possible. I would attempt to console the Kellers from halfway around the world if such a thing was possible.

"George, thank you for coming," Annabel finished. "Thank you for bringing us your messages from Michael."

That night, I slept in Michael's apartment. At four in the morning, I awoke and sat upright in bed, as if after a morning cup of coffee. Markus slumbered while adrenalin flooded my system.

I sensed Michael was around. He was in the room. He seemed to be calling to me to pay attention—a strange entreaty but coming from where? I had the feeling he wanted to talk. The voice was back. "I'm going to appear to you *all*—I'm going to find a way to come back." The tone seemed almost childlike, like that of a willful, playful little boy. I lay there waiting. I shut my eyes.

Suddenly I saw yellow pinpoints of light shoot past me to the right. The image was similar to the image you see when you close your eyes and press against your eyelids with your knuckles. I could see a strange glow, but only in one spot appearing in front of me, then it whizzed off to the right, then to the left. As soon as a light would appear in front of me, from behind my closed eyelids, it would take off past me like a jet.

This phenomenon went on for several moments until a startling thing happened: I saw first the outline of a face, then the clear image of a face with eyes looking into mine. As it came more into focus, I saw it was the face of Michael Keller.

It was as if he was giving me a light show in spirit. Over and over, the image of his face illuminated this strange realm of darkness behind my closed eyelids, only to dissolve into hundreds of tiny points of light.

This event went on for at least twenty minutes, Michael reappearing from different points. Each image of his face was different in perspective, becoming more animated and lifelike every time it reconstituted itself.

Suddenly the thought came to my mind: "Put your hand up against the wall."

Strange request. I did so, and I could feel a heartbeat.

I took my hand away, thinking that it was the sensation of my own heartbeat flooding through the capillaries in the palm of my hand. I adjusted my weight to make sure that this wasn't the case. I sat up, and slowly moved my hand to the wall, paying attention to my own heartbeat as I touched the wall. And there it was again! A heartbeat. Strong, with an even rhythm.

After a few moments, I lay back in bed, confounded and amazed at what had happened.

I closed my eyes, and then more strongly than before, the light show resumed, this time with Michael's face seeming to materialize as if pressed through some substance from another dimension.

It was then that I could hear his voice again, as I did on June 28th in my apartment in Los Angeles. He sent me the thought, "I will appear for *all* of you!"

It appeared that if this communication was genuine, then Michael could be put to the test. We could expect more communications from him, and not a disconnection.

I asked of him in my mind, "What do you mean? Are you saying that you're going to physically appear?"

Suddenly, the image dissolved into a hundred points of light, and I opened my eyes to see the purple-blue streaks of the Frankfurt sunrise.

He didn't answer. He just echoed the same phrase several times as I lay down to try to catch another hour's sleep. "I will appear for *all* of you!"

In the morning, Thorsten stopped at Michael's apartment to say goodbye. He had to go to work, and could not see me off at the airport.

"That poor girl last night." He was referring to Ulla, having observed her trauma. "Now you see why I did this Catholic ritual. She should see a priest."

"What's a priest going to do for her?" I asked.

"Wait till he takes something of yours!" Thorsten cautioned.

I laughed.

"By the way, I'm glad you're here to give Markus a hand, he looks like he could use it," I said. "If he discusses suicidal thoughts with you, help him. Please make sure he seeks professional help."

"I'll do my best," he said. "Soon, I will move from this apartment building. I'm beginning to think that it's haunted—not just by Michael," he said.

He stood before me now, and teared up a bit. What was there to say?

"I'll keep you posted when I get back to the United States," I said. "Take care of yourself."

"Do what *you* can for Markus before you leave," he finished.

Markus accompanied me to the airport via the subway. I felt a strange mixture of sadness and elation. The trip to Frankfurt had only seemed to create new questions rather than answer the ones I brought to Germany. At the airport, Markus and I stopped at Harrods to do some last minute shopping, then settled at the bar outside the gate at Continental. Then Markus addressed me.

"I don't know. I just—so hard, you know? The day before the accident, in the car with Angelina, uhhhh! Michael, and I—we had an argument—so bad. I think on it, and it makes me sad."

Angelina met with me briefly the day before my departure, but remained silent about the details surrounding Michael's death. As we parted company, she stated, "We'll talk about it when I come to America to visit you," but she gave no date when she planned to arrive.

"You tried your best to help him, Markus." I tried to reassure him.

"I know, I know. But it's . . ." The two had not left off on a good note, then Michael was dead.

"Markus, what do you think of these messages, and Ulla's earring? Do you believe that Michael is doing these things?"

He shook his head. "No."

"I've wanted to tell you that I believe he's safe. I've never been able to say that with certainty about anyone I know who's died. But I think he's safe, Markus. I know it hurts, but he sent that message about the jacket for you." I proceeded to explain it again.

"I don't believe all of this. It's . . . not possible."

We paused. An awkward silence.

Tears welled up in Markus' eyes. "You know . . . some-time I think, he . . . it is better. The place. Sometimes I think, I want to go there and leave this place."

"Are you saying that you believe he is somewhere else?" I asked.

"I . . . don't know. I only know I don't like this place right now."

I was alarmed that Markus might be having suicidal thoughts.

"Markus . . . all this is going to pass. This is a terrible loss, but all crises are temporary. I hope you understand that it's important to get help and support, and work your feelings out with a mental health professional if you have to."

Could he even understand my English, I wondered?

His red eyes seemed to glow momentarily. He looked at his watch. "You'll miss your plane."

A few moments later, I turned to Markus as I loaded my bags onto the conveyer belt. What irony, I thought to myself. Counseling the man Michael had been living with, the Michael who had been my partner for several years.

"Thank you, George." Markus stood there as I passed through the metal detector and crowds gathered between us, milling hurriedly around.

Moments later, I looked, and he was gone. So I left Germany, worried about the welfare of those Michael had left behind, as the phenomenon of his afterlife existence continued to grow.

Chapter Ten

ADCs with Ulla

"It doesn't stop. It's just the beginning."

—Ulla Simic in a letter to me from August 1996

The psychologist Carl Jung used the term synchronicity, a principle best described as "meaningful coincidence in human affairs." To Jung, synchronicity defied rational explanation, and continues to be an unexplainable circumstance in which outward events that appear accidental or coincidental may be meaningful and connected. Ulla's and my experiences seemed to transcend mere coincidences. They appeared to fit the defined parameters of ADCs and may well have been a part of an effort on the part of the spirit of Michael Keller to continue to communicate with us.

A few days after my return to L.A., I felt a strange sensation like a presence in the apartment.[1] I noticed a light in my study flickering on and off. I walked over and screwed the bulb in tightly, then backed up. The flickering continued. I checked for confirmation and said out loud,

"Michael: If that's you, turn the light on and off three times." I watched in amazement as it blinked on and off three times, then stopped. I observed that it never blinked again.

I walked into my bedroom, and tried the same experiment with a light on my chest of drawers.

"Michael: Try this one." Again, the light blinked clearly on and off three times, then nothing. Neither the bulb in my study nor the bulb in the bedroom was broken, and neither flickered on and off again. What was most odd was the electrical disturbance coupled with the keen sensing of Michael's presence.

One night, I had a vivid dream of a reunion with Michael.[2] He appeared as an adult, exactly as I had remembered him. Unusual in its vivid candor, this dream bore the distinct experience of being like the waking state, and I felt Michael's presence as if there had been no accident, and no death.

We were sitting casually in a room in "heaven," talking at great length, when I turned to say that it was time for us to return to Hollywood. Suddenly, we were standing at the front door of my apartment. Michael hesitated, as if to say he couldn't come all the way from *there* to *here*, as I, somehow, went through the door of the apartment.

I turned to look from within my apartment, and he was knocking at the door. In reality, I found myself beneath my sheets, back in bed, and heard real knocking at the door as I awoke. I paused, listened, and realized that the knocking continued. It was 3 A.M.

I went to the door and opened it. No one was there.

I walked down the hallway and looked down the stairs and saw no one. I returned to my apartment and looked out the window. No one was leaving the building, which has a security door.

The next day, I asked the building's custodian, Sarkis Zabounian, if the security door had been locked. He assured me that no one had entered the building at that hour.

That night, like clockwork, Ulla called. I hadn't told her about the dream or the knocking. She'd called to relay another supernatural experience with Michael's spirit.

"You can't believe it, but last night Michael came to me in a dream—came right up to my front door and started knocking!" She related.

The bond between Ulla and myself continued to grow. She relayed information back and forth to the Kellers, and became a link between us. We spoke frequently in the months following Michael's death, despite the fact that our phone bills mounted.

After-death communications were so new for us that we kept to ourselves during this time. On July 29, 1996, Ulla wrote me the following letter:

George:

It doesn't stop, it's just the beginning.

Talking to you, and being connected with you in a certain way, is a very comfortable feeling for me. Michael's death has certainly changed my life.

I finally realize that all this love I held inside for so many years I can give away now. Love is the key. He gives me this present. And I'm glad that I woke up. I treasure him in my heart. My feelings towards Michael are stranger than ever. Night is breaking in, my best time to hear Michael.

I love you always,

Ulla

On September 4, I came home to discover that my alarm clock had been moved from the floor by my bed,[3] and placed squarely in the center of my bed's comforter. At first I thought the apartment had been burglarized, and went to Sarkis to ask if he or any one else had entered the apartment in my absence. He noted that the only person who had the keys to my apartment was our eighty-seven-year-old landlady who lived on the first floor of our building. "Mary has asthma and can barely make out the front door," he informed me. "And I wasn't in your apartment," he added.

Ulla called the next day after flying back on Lufthansa from Havana, Cuba. She recounted that in the middle of the night in her hotel room she again felt the overwhelming presence of Michael's spirit. While she was asleep, her battery-operated Braun alarm clock went off autonomously. A thorough examination revealed that the clock was neither broken nor set to go off at 3 A.M.

"The only thing I'm sure of," Ulla related, "was that it had to do with Michael. I feel he set the alarm off!"

It was then that I told her that my alarm clock had been placed on my bed in my absence, and that my custodian denied anyone had entered my apartment that day.

"This is getting scary!" she affirmed.

Over two months had passed since Michael's death, the time allotted to a "normal" bereavement period according to the *DSM-IV* (the diagnostic manual used by mental health professionals). Ulla and I were experiencing an increase in after-death communications, not a decrease or cessation of them.

A few weeks later, Ulla flew as a flight attendant on Lufthansa to Puerto Rico. She related an ADC that got her attention:

I checked in at the hotel in San Juan, Puerto Rico; I went up to my room, got changed, ready to meet up with the crew for drinks. I went in the lift, alone, and the elevator got stuck.

Me, all by myself. Then suddenly, I panicked. I felt Michael. He was with me. I pushed the alarm button, nobody could hear me.

I started screaming. No answer! Then, out of the blue, the lift went down. I called the engineer to check the elevator—everything was O.K., he reassured me. He couldn't find a technical defect or problem!

Whether it was from Ulla or myself, the information that "something had happened" and was linked to Michael continued to reach Annabel and Ludwig in Germany. They were shocked, but because two people were reporting shared ADC experiences, they began to share the conviction that Michael's spirit appeared to be close at hand and eager to communicate his continued existence.

Rather than extend the bereavement process, these calls seemed to have a therapeutic effect and the Kellers gratefully acknowledged the reporting of the ADCs. They also began to wonder if Michael's "travels" would take him home to Germany to bring an ADC experience for them, for if these experiences were real, it made perfect sense that Michael's parents would eventually have experiences of their own.

Neither Ulla nor myself knew anyone who had experienced these kinds of phenomena, and there were times when the unpredictability of Michael's "visits" became an intimidating and overwhelming drama for Ulla.

She wrote me many letters, expressing mixed emotions:

I have found it very difficult to find someone who doesn't think I'm crazy because I got gifted.

In another, she wrote:

George, I never asked for something unique like this is, but it found me! A tiny little thing like me. That huge, enormous power wanted me. In a way, I'm overwhelmed.

Yet another milestone occurred in September 1996 when Heiko called me from Germany to confirm that an insurance policy had paid out a substantial sum of money by mail to the Kellers, courtesy of Lufthansa.

Just when things seemed to begin to stabilize, Ulla fell into crisis. At the end of September, I received the following letter from her:

George, I have some bad news. Condor[4] wrote a letter to me, and they want me to see a therapist. My boss has the impression that I'm not well, and I should talk. I was in tears. Is this what I deserve after helping out so many others? I'm totally down, because this event will probably hold me back from becoming a purser or change to another airline. Perhaps this will be written down in my file! The therapist is from Lufthansa and my appointment is on Tuesday, September 24th.

One of the fleet managers will be there too. I know, I don't have to go there or can refuse to say a word if I don't want to, but I think it makes the situation worse. What would you say?

Ulla had been referred to Dr. Roland Kulhanek, just as Michael had been in June 1996. She asked me to draft and fax a letter of support to Dr. Kulhanek prior to their appointment. I advocated that Ulla's experiences be taken at face value, and I stated that it was my clinical impression that Ulla did not appear to be suffering from bereavement delusions or hallucinations.

Just prior to faxing the letter, I stood up from my PC and walked into my bedroom to discover my alarm clock giving off an almost imperceptibly soft, tiny succession of beeps. A moment passed when I realized that it was not my imagination. The beeps progressed, getting louder.

I picked it up and examined it. The alarm was neither broken, nor was it set to go off, and yet it was ringing, just as Ulla's Braun had been set off autonomously in Havana.

Chapter Eleven

Morticia

"My children will be very cosmopolitan, and they should learn early about the world and its—cosmetics."

—Michael Keller in a letter to me from January 1994

Michael's colleague Angelina Usai never gave a reason for visiting me in October 1996. She called and left a message to announce her arrival.

"Darling! I have some time off. I come on Lufthansa and arrive at LAX on October 11 at 10:35 P.M. *your time*. I must go feed Aphrodite now. Ciao!"

Aphrodite is Angelina's pet tarantula.

In truth, I saw this visit as a crucial opportunity not only to lend support to Michael's former colleague, but also to find out the facts about what led up to the tragedy of Michael's death from Angelina, who had been with Michael the day before he died.

Holst's "The Planets" played on my car stereo as I approached LAX to pick up Angelina. The spooky score reached its climax with "Neptune: The Mystic," as I parked the car.

I greeted Angelina as she swept down the escalator in a black ensemble that called to mind Michael's nickname for her: "Morticia Adams."

"Darling!" She gave me a healthy, prolonged kiss as we reached the ground level. I pulled back and looked. Despite the dark circles under her eyes, she had the same dramatic energy I remembered from our dinner in Frankfurt.

"I'm so glad to get out of Germany!" she confessed, as she draped her garment bag over my shoulder. "These Lufthansa supervisors are trying to get *me* to go to Dr. Kulhanek, just like Ulla." She launched into a tirade of righteous indignation as we headed toward the baggage claim area. "Poor Ulla! They don't give either of us a choice, really. They assume we're upset about Michael, and that we need to talk it out."

Clearly, she was deeply depressed, though cleverly disguising the fact with humor and confidence.

"How is Markus?" I asked, fearing the worst.

"Oh, he has already met another man." She gave me a cold stare of disbelief.

"That was quick," I added. "I worried that he might be suicidal a few months ago." I couldn't believe that Reicher could already be involved again.

"No one can believe it," she added.

Apparently, rather than process the tragedy of Michael's death, Markus had simply moved on, found another partner, and moved out of the Toengesgasse apartment, putting the past behind him with a geographic move.

"And Ulla? Did she keep her job?" I hadn't heard from Ulla in weeks.

"Of course, darling! They just told her, 'Stop talking about the ghost of Michael Keller to your colleagues, and do your job.'"

Switching gears, she became quite serious. "I miss him," Angelina said point blank as we left the airport. "It's like somebody stabbed me in the heart."

I had my work cut out for me.

When we reached my apartment, we called Ulla in Germany. She sounded agitated, and there was static on the line between us. We wondered if Michael was somehow responsible for this electrical disturbance, so I said aloud: "Michael—if this is you, please stop." This seemed to silence the arpeggio of telephone beeps.

Angelina sat in the living room eavesdropping on our conversation, looking at me like I was crazy.

"My God!" Ulla exclaimed. "Let me tell you the latest: he kept setting off my alarm clock, and I got sick of it, so I went and bought a new alarm clock. Another Braun. Tonight, I drew a bath and right before you called, I'm sitting there having a bubble bath, and the alarm went off again. I can't believe it! A new alarm clock!"

I asked for clarification: "He set off the old alarm when it wasn't set to go off. It wasn't broken, so you bought a new alarm clock, and now he's set *that* one off?" I said this loud enough for Angelina to hear.

"Ja!" Ulla responded. She was scared. If she couldn't control when Michael did these things, how could it ever stop? "What do I do?" she begged.

"Just say out loud, 'Michael—stop!' Like I just did with the phone static. I think it's an attention getter, if anything."

She seemed to take my advice. "O.K. I'll try," she sighed.

I handed the phone to Angelina, hopeful that Ulla would report Michael's latest event and that Angelina would see that maybe the two of us weren't so crazy after all. Angelina immediately changed the subject.

The next morning, I announced our itinerary.

"Angelina! We're going to 'do Hollywood' today—you name it. The sky's the limit! Anything you want. You want to go put your footprints in Mann's Chinese, we're going to do the footprint thing at Mann's Chinese." I wanted to indulge her like a child.

She came bounding back into the living room with a stick of lip liner. "I wonder if I can use this lip liner?" She showed me a lip liner a girlfriend had left in my bathroom. "I lost my lip liner, it disappeared after we came back from the airport," she added.

"Of course," I answered. "Are you ready for the Walk of Fame?" I asked.

"First things first!" she warned, as she applied her make-up. "First, we go to a supermarket where I can buy some good cosmetics, because this lip liner melts too fast, I can tell already. It will last until we get to the store—that's all."

For Angelina, a first trip through Hollywood carried with it the fantasy of being discovered and escaping from reality.

After a preliminary trip to Von's for lip liner, we made a stop at another supermarket on Hillhurst. Spotting a refrigerated flower section, Angelina extracted a dozen white roses, walked with me to the register, paid for the flowers and handed them to me.

"For you, darling! You know, Michael's favorite were white roses."

"I didn't know that," I responded.

"Oh, yes. His favorite." She lifted the blossoms to her nose, taking in their fragrance. Afterwards, we returned to the apartment to drop off the groceries. Angelina cut the stems of the white roses and put them in a vase which she placed on a coffee table in my living room. We turned around and headed back to Vermont Avenue.

In homage to Michael, Angelina assumed the persona of Marlene Dietrich as we drove, beckoning: "Dietrich must get to Paramount Studios at once!"

She popped the passenger seat mirror down, dusted it off with a Kleenex and began to do her make-up while I rolled down the windows.

"And please put down the convertible top. Fresh air will add luster to Dietrich's complexion!" Angelina stared with humorous gratification, her deep-set brown eyes widening with anticipation of exploring Hollywood.

"We will get into Paramount, I promise," I responded, and put in a 1930s tape of Dietrich singing *Falling in Love Again* while I lowered the top of my convertible and drove off.

Angelina applied magenta lipstick as she reached into her purse and rummaged around for a moment.

Suddenly, her tone changed completely. "Damnit. I can't find that lip liner that we bought this morning. I put it here somewhere. I know it's in here." She continued to search the bag as we made our way down the street.

"I can't find it! I have to have lip liner!" Like a child, she looked at me for support, sat back and folded her arms.

"What's the big deal? I'll buy you another lip liner on the way back, O.K.?"

She seemed strangely agitated. "Oh, but I know I put it

in here." She continued to search the bag, pulling things out and placing them on her lap as we turned onto Western. A few moments later, we pulled up to another supermarket, and I ran in, bought a second lip liner pencil, and popped back out to the car.

"Now take this lip liner, and I will watch as you zip it up into your bag. You're not going to lose it again. O.K.?" I was firm.

Angelina followed my instructions: zip, done. The lip liner was now zipped into the inner pocket of her purse.

As we sped off for Paramount Studios, I popped in the tape of Marlene Dietrich to get us in the mood.

We pulled up to the Paramount lot to discover that a cement gate now blocks off the entrance that Dietrich once used. In addition, there was a private reception going on in the theater adjacent to the studio entrance.

I parked the car down a side street, and announced, "I've got an idea. We're both dressed up, why not just act like we're going to this reception? Who knows—maybe we'll run into some real celebrities instead of their footprints . . ."

"Darling . . . I don't know." Angelina demurred.

"Look! You've come all the way from Germany—we're going into that studio!" I grabbed Angelina by the hand and we crossed the busy intersection and walked past the first gate. The security guard waved us on without asking for I.D. Settling by the grand fountain outside the original Paramount gate, I began snapping photos as Angelina posed as Dietrich on the first day of shooting of *The Blue Angel*.

Our next stop was Mann's Chinese Theater. Angelina ran past me, down Hollywood Boulevard, her black cape billowing in the breeze, to stop to look at the twin stars on the Walk of Fame in front of the entrance: "Look! It's the star of Barbra Streisand!" She stood in awe outside the cement-studded foyer of Mann's like a child at the gate to Disneyland.

She ran into the courtyard. "Tom Cruise! I can't believe it! Please. You must take a picture," she cooed. Crouching and putting her hands in the cement, she turned and smiled as I snapped away. "Tom Cruise put his hands here, I don't believe it."

Angelina sank her heels into one footprint after another. First on Marilyn Monroe, then on Elizabeth Taylor as I looked on and took more photos.

At a nearby gift shop, Angelina purchased two "make-your-own" Hollywood stars for the Walk of Fame, and presented me with the kit as we walked across the street to have dinner.

"It's good to see you so happy," I said. The dark circles under Angelina's eyes were now complemented by a weak smile and rosy complexion—a welcome transformation.

We sipped iced teas, and proceeded to spell out our names with tiny gold letters on the cardboard replicas of Hollywood Walk of Fame stars. I juxtaposed Michael Keller's initials, "MCK," above my name, and affixed the "K" just as Angelina completed her star.

She held it up: it read, "MORTICIA."

"Aphrodite will be so impressed," I goaded.

Angelina reached for her purse.

"This has been the best day I've had since this whole stupid tragedy happened!" She was grateful.

She smiled as she opened her compact and applied more lipstick.

"I feel glamorous, so—I want to go press my body into that cement, and then everyone can take a picture of the world famous Angelina Usai at Mann's Chinese!" She unzipped the compartment in her purse.

"Now—let's see that lip liner," I asked.

She looked into the compartment and turned pale.

"What's wrong?" I asked.

"Oh, my God! It's gone again!"

"It can't be," I said, and looked into the empty compartment, then into her wide eyes.

"He's taken my lip liner!" she finished.

Our Hollywood outing seemed to end with an ADC, with reality interrupting our fantasy. At home, Angelina seemed preoccupied and depressed, and we sat in silence for a nearly an hour. Finally, she spoke. "Those last two months, everything just started going crazy, those last two months before he died." She was referring to the months of April and May 1996.

"Michael started canceling trips. He was the purser, and you can't do that! In June, he didn't even call the airline. They were ready to leave, and he didn't show up, didn't call—nothing. It was more than just the partying—it was a major change in his behavior."

She lit a cigarette, and played with the ice bobbing in her glass of white wine. "One night, during those last two months, he went to a restaurant with Markus and Michael's parents. They sat down to eat dinner. He was quiet, hardly said a word. Then, when the dinners got there, he excused himself from the table, and just . . . disappeared!"

Emotion began to well up in Angelina. Clearly this was

agitating her, but she had to get it out. I was curious to learn more about what happened during Michael's last two months, as he and I had fallen out of communication during the time I prepared to move to Hollywood and drive cross country.

"Where did he go?" I asked.

"No one knows. No one. He was missing for three days, and then, finally, he just walks back into the apartment like nothing had happened. He didn't say a word. Nothing. He was disoriented from the flights, from the time changes, and the coke." She smoked her cigarette down to the butt.

"Do you think that he knew he was going to die?" I asked. "A premonition or something like that?"

"Yes—and I don't understand it. Then, the day before the accident Michael called me and said that he and Markus were going to Mainz, and asked if I would join them. I didn't want to! I never knew what to expect at this point. I said 'No,' but he just begged me. I agreed because he insisted, and, and, *and*—we went to Mainz and were driving back in his Cabriolet with the top down. Michael was wearing this hat that he loved. Well, the wind picked up, and before he could catch it, the hat flew out of the car.

"He told Markus to stop, but Markus ignored him, like he wasn't even listening. Again, Michael said to stop, but nothing, and so Michael just started screaming at him to stop the car, and finally Markus pulls off the road. Needless to say, I'm regretting that I went after all, but—what a mess."

She paused, and took a sip of wine, anxious to get this off of her chest. Then she continued: "So we stopped on the shoulder of the road, and Markus went into the traffic to get this hat. Well, cars had run over it, of course, and when Michael saw that it was dirty, he just—it was the last straw, as you say. He let Markus have it: 'You don't respect me, you don't care about my things, you wear my hats, you wear my jackets . . .'

"Yes. He said that. 'You wear my jackets, you don't take care of my things!' He was so pissed. He took the car keys from the ignition, and threw them into the stinging nettle bushes off the roadway. It was dark, and there was so many bushes. The more we looked for the keys, the more we got stung by those bushes. It was awful.

"Michael knew his life was out of control. He started walking in and out of the traffic that night. He could have died that night! Then, it was a whole scene: everyone was there—Heiko Keller, and his parents. Someone called his parents on a cell phone, and the Kellers arrived with a spare car key. We were all there, with the headlights pointing in the darkness, next to the highway. It was so sad. He just sat there next to the road with me, crying like a little boy. It was the first time I saw Michael cry, and it was the last time I saw Michael alive."

Clearly, Michael's use of stimulants had heightened his mood, and the accident the next day seemed to become a self-fulfilling prophesy for him.

"Do you think he committed suicide?" I asked.

"No. I don't." She looked me right in the eye.

I was relieved. Regardless of what I may have intuited from Michael's messages, I valued Angelina's honest opinion.

"Let me ask you this. You know that Ulla and I are still experiencing strange things—'messages from Michael'— and, after tonight, I have to ask: Have you had any experiences like ours that you want to talk about?"

"No . . . nothing." Angelina looked down at the floor, then fumed. "I don't believe all of this life-after-death nonsense! I don't! You're born, you live, you die . . . *basta!*" She clapped her hands. At that, all the electricity went out in my apartment.

When I went outside to investigate, I discovered that mine was the only apartment of twelve units to lose power. Back in the apartment, I sat watching the glow of Angelina's cigarette in the dark. We were speechless.

By the end of her visit, we both felt relieved of some of our mixed feelings surrounding Michael's death. We both wished there was something we could have done to prevent his death, but we knew that somehow it had been beyond our control. The impending doom that seemed to haunt him, and the stimulants that had made his life unmanageable, were now a thing of the past. Michael had moved on.

When we awoke at 4 A.M. on the day of her departure, Angelina rose like an automaton, rushed around the apartment, throwing cosmetics hastily into bags, and stuffing gifts I'd bought for Ulla into the last empty compartment in her suitcase. Without having breakfast, we were off to LAX in the early morning semilight.

In the airport lounge, Angelina piped up, "Say goodbye to *Otze!*" She pulled a stuffed kangaroo out of the bag and sat it next to her coffee. Otze belonged to Michael, and had been given to Angelina by the Keller family in June.

I addressed the stuffed animal: "Not to have martinis on the way back to Frankfurt! You're going to give your mother a heart attack!"

Angelina laughed.

I worried that she might use quick remedies for time changes like Michael.

"No more cocktails for Otze." Angelina agreed. She hugged the animal to her chest, and we kissed. I took a long look into her eyes as tears welled up.

"I say, the worst is over. Now is the time for healing."

We walked hand in hand to the gate.

"One last thing," I said, just before she boarded the plane. "Do you believe that Michael is safe?"

She gave her flight pass to the Lufthansa ground attendant.

"Let's just say that I'm agnostic at this point." She kissed me goodbye, waved Otze's little stuffed hand, teared up, turned dramatically on her heel, and marched into the cabin of the Lufthansa jet as the doors closed behind her.

Chapter Twelve

The Rose Petal Angel

"Many spirit people are able to influence the electrical field of protons and electrons and effect changes. . . ."

—James Van Praagh, *Talking to Heaven*

October 17, 1996

Had Michael turned off the electricity and caused the disappearance of Angelina's lip liner?

The most confusing aspect of these strange experiences was that there was no way of proving whether an ADC was due to the faulty wiring in my apartment or to the spirit of Michael Keller. Interpreting what was communicated, if anything, was becoming a confusing aspect of these ADCs.

There was no physical evidence of Michael's visits, no visible proof of his life after death, and so as Angelina slept in Lufthansa's business class on the evening of October 17, 1996, I sat at my computer staring at my diary of these strange events.

I was depressed. I had found a great love in knowing

Michael, only to have it squelched and erased by a couple of cars . . . and now, what was I to make of all this?

I cleaned my apartment, and at 11:00 P.M., I moved from my office into the living room and tried to watch TV, surfing the channels without settling long on anything.

I stared instead at Angelina's dozen white roses blooming in the center of my coffee table. Consoled by her visit, I crawled into bed and covered my head with the sheets still permeated with her fragrance. Crazy world, I thought.

Around 3 A.M., I was awakened by the alarm clock. I rolled over and shut it off. At the time, I assumed I must have set it for a nap and left the alarm in the "on" position by mistake. But could it be Michael again? Waking me up in the middle of the night? When he was alive, he would call in the middle of the night.

Flicking on the overhead light, I held up the alarm. Now, I could see that it was set for 11 A.M. I discovered also that the alarm knob was set in the "on" position as if I had never turned it off just a minute before. I popped out of bed and headed to the living room. The moment I entered, I noticed what looked like a torn sheet of paper in the corner of the room.

I bent down to take a look: it was one of Angelina's white roses. Upon closer examination, I saw that the flower head had been severed from its stem and that the petals were spread all over the place. The rest of the roses remained where I had left them the night before—in the vase on the coffee table in my living room seven feet from where I was crouching.

This was not an accidental event, a rose falling out of a vase onto the floor. Someone had put it in the corner of my room.

"God almighty," I said out loud.

I couldn't believe it. I walked over to the vase on the coffee table; it was then that I saw that a path of white rose petals led from the vase to the petals on the floor. Every foot or so, another rose petal led the way back to the now-only eleven roses on the table.

I assumed someone had broken into the apartment. I hurriedly walked to the front door and found that it was locked and double-bolted. Next, I went to the phone and called Angelina, who had just arrived in Germany at noon, her time. I cut to the chase.

"I have to ask you: Did you pull out one of your roses and put it into the corner of my living room before you left yesterday?" Angelina had been the only one in my apartment since we left for the airport the previous morning.

"Darling, of course not! You know what a rush I was in to leave. I bought those roses for *you*, darling! Don't be silly!" She was definite.

"Are you sure? I mean, I just woke up, and one of the roses is lying on the floor and the petals are all over the place."

She became quiet. "I fixed the roses in the vase, and that is where I left them."

"Sorry to wake you," I said. "I'm going to bed now, and I'll call you when I get up."

"*Alles liebe*. I love you. Be well."

Of course it wasn't Angelina.

I was shocked. The roses were fresh, just beginning to bloom. The only way the petals could have made it from the bulb to the floor would have been if someone or *something* pulled them out. I walked to the coffee table and shook each of the rest of the roses in the vase to see if the petals were loose. Not a petal fell.

I walked back to the corner of my living room where the petal arrangement now lay. I picked up the bulb of the rose and examined the base; it was a fresh separation, and looked like it had been pulled from the stem not an hour before. It did not look as if it had been cut by a knife.

I looked at the arrangement of petals on the floor, wondering how they got there, and what was the point of all this. This pondering bolstered my mood. I was excited. Carrying the stem and bulb back into the bedroom, I placed them on my chest of drawers, and went back to bed. It appeared that finally Michael had given me the evidence that I wanted.

First thing in the morning, I headed to the store for film. Once home, I shot a roll of pictures of the petal phenomenon. Now I could have photographs of one of Michael's *messages*.

As I left the building to drop the film off to be developed, I passed Sarkis, the building's custodian, and decided to keep this latest event a secret. Still, I couldn't help but ask, jokingly, "Weren't in my apartment last night, were you?"

He sprayed me with the hose.

"Just checking," I added.

That evening, as I stared at the photographs, I noticed that the petal formation included two petals placed in the top right corner of the room facing my office. Though it is hard to describe, something struck me almost immediately: Whoever had done this appeared to be right-handed. I am left-handed, but Michael was right-handed. And what of the white petals leading from the vase and coffee table to the arrangement on the floor? Placed there deliberately.

It is important to note that the petal arrangement

appeared directly behind my office and the seat where I was keeping a journal of my ADC experiences that would later lead me to write this book. Was this intended as an endorsement for writing this book?

Later that evening, a close friend, Rachel Sparer, called from New York while I sat studying the pictures, and I was candid and open with her about what happened.

"Does it look like it has some sort of a pattern?" she asked.

"I'm so shocked that things are moving around in my apartment I haven't given it serious thought."

While I spoke to her, I held a photo of the rose petal arrangement up to the light and traced the outline with a Montblanc pen that Michael had given me as a present in South Florida.

I nearly dropped the phone.

"Rachel, I just traced this thing and—God."

"What?" She panicked.

I took a deep breath.

"Rachel. It looks . . . like an *angel*."

Chapter Thirteen

Home for the Holidays

"In spirit form, you can always contact those that are in the physical state if you choose to."

—Brian Weiss, M.D., *Many Lives, Many Masters*

My life became filled with ironies and opposites.

By day, a steady stream of clients were requesting medicine at my clinic to "make the voices stop," and at any given point I would open my own sixth sense to hear what Michael might be sending out, for the messages continued.

In Heinrich Mann's novel, *Professor Unrath*, upon which the film *The Blue Angel* was based, the main character is a teacher who resigns from his position and takes an unconventional path which leads to his downfall. Sometimes I worried about the direction I had chosen as a mental health professional who dabbles with mediumship and ADCs. Where was all this leading?

Michael's thirtieth birthday on November 23 was looming ahead like a strange milestone. Meanwhile, I was stuck in one of L.A.'s infamous traffic jams when I heard that little voice in my head go off again, for the first time since my trip to Frankfurt. "The ring," it said. "Tell them about the ring."

"What about the ring?" I was open-minded. Elaborate, please. Translate.

"They fixed it."

"What ring?" I asked.

"*My* ring—the lapis one, the blue one. The one with the Keller family crest. They fixed the ring this month."

The information was so specific, and the tone imperative and unrelenting.

I knew the ring he was talking about. Michael *always* wore it, even five months ago, the night he was killed. I remembered that Heiko had told me that the ring was badly damaged in the accident.

Why would the family fix this ring? Michael's body was buried, so what would be the point of such a thing? Perhaps he was buried with it. Common sense made this message seem absurd.

Still, I took a chance the next time I spoke with Annabel, the night before Michael's birthday. "Annabel—I have another message." I held my breath.

"What is it?" she asked.

"Michael says you fixed the ring this month."

"That's true! We just got it back from the jewelers! The gold had been bent, and the stone lost." She was jubilant.

"Share the news with Ludwig," I urged.

"It's his birthday, and he says *hello* to us," Annabel added and started to cry. "I can't believe it."

It was uncanny how the messages continued even when I wasn't thinking about Michael Keller. I was looking for something in the kitchen when I again felt that strange feeling of being summoned. My thoughts were pushed aside by Michael's spirit. The voice was back!

"There's a tractor in the cemetery."

"What tractor in the cemetery?"

"The one my mother hates."

"Why does your mother hate the tractor in the cemetery?"

This was like dialogue from *What's Up, Doc?* Michael's favorite movie.

"Because it's there day after day, and they won't move it. Tell her I told you about the tractor in the cemetery, and she'll know it's me and that I see her there."

Both Ludwig and Annabel continued to go to the cemetery every day to pray, take flowers, and be near Michael. Sometimes they went to the cemetery two or three times in one day. I called to pass on the message.

"Froliche Wienachten!" I heard Ludwig say on the other end. He sounded surprisingly upbeat.

"Merry Christmas!" I said, affirming that it was good to hear him in good spirits again.

"Well, you know, we were at the cemetery today and we said 'hello' to Michael in the heavens. We know he is O.K. Sometimes I feel he stands behind me at work and says *hello*. I feel his spirit there." Then he put Annabel on.

"George, I say, thank you very much—thank you for all you do. We think it's great that you can speak with Michael, and it makes us so happy." She began to cry.

"Annabel—I think Michael sent a Christmas message." Again, a big swallow, gulp, and out with it. "He says to tell you that there's been a tractor in the cemetery, and it's there day after day, and you want it removed."

"Yes! There was a tractor in the cemetery in late November, and just this month! They just let it sit there, it was so ugly. I called the Burgermeister of Kirschfurt to have it removed!"

On New Year's Eve, I lay down to take a nap, but I couldn't fall asleep. Suddenly, I sensed Michael's presence and heard the chatter again.

"Where are you?" I asked.

"Here." He answered.

"In my bedroom?"

"Yes. Happy New Year. Thank you for your help."

"Michael, what you really need to do is go to Germany and do something directly for your parents. This is all so confusing for me. You need to go home, and do something. Sometimes I wonder if you're really here and if all of this is really happening."

"I'm here. You don't believe me?"

"I'm skeptical." I got up out of bed to go to the bathroom.

When I returned, I discovered that my alarm clock was sitting squarely in the middle of the bed. It had been moved from the floor to the bed again, just like in September of 1996.

In Kirschfurt, a few days after New Year's, the Kellers' Christmas tree was still standing. Interspersed with ornaments and tinsel were photos of Michael, along with black ribbons—this had been their first Christmas without him.

Annabel was in the living room having coffee when suddenly, she heard what she thought were two beeps. She got up, and walked to the dinner table where Michael's travel alarm clock rested on display. She and Ludwig had placed it there after Ulla and I described our alarm clock phenomena, in case Michael wanted to communicate with them by setting it off.

Through the fall months, the clock just sat there, ticking away. The battery hadn't run down; it was still keeping good time. Now, she knew she had heard something. Beep. Beep.

Annabel stood up, and called loudly for Ludwig, who was just coming in from the office. "Did you hear that?" she asked him.

"Maybe," he answered, tentatively.

As they both stood before the dining room table, the alarm clock went off again, two soft beeps.

Beep. Beep.

"Could it be?" Annabel asked.

They looked at each other, and started to cry.

In February of 1997, just when Ludwig and Annabel seemed to be moving closer into acceptance with Michael's passing, a new crisis struck in Kirschfurt.

Driving home after meeting with his parents to leave flowers at the site of Michael's accident, Heiko Keller was nearly killed in an automobile accident.

As Heiko made his way to Laudenbach, a Turkish couple in a drag race with a friend collided with Heiko head-on going over a hundred miles per hour. The driver was killed on impact, and his girlfriend later died in ICU.

The crash totaled Heiko's car, and he had to be extracted from the auto by the "jaws of life." He later told me he had had a near-death experience.

"It was the most beautiful experience—I felt like all cares had left me, all desires, and in their place, I felt the most wonderful sense of satisfaction. Just indescribable. No, I didn't see Michael, or any angels or anything like that, but as this world seemed to fade into the shadows, I felt myself drawn like so many people have said, through a rainbow tunnel of light, and the light itself seemed alive, caring, loving.

"As I prepared to leave this world, I saw my whole life like a movie. Then there was an interruption: I remember someone kept shouting my name over and over again. It was a local police officer I knew, who was trying to keep me conscious on the way to the hospital. Suddenly I was back in my body, and I hated it. I was ready to leave. I was at peace." Heiko was glad to be alive, but if he had to go, he felt ready and welcome.

"Somehow," Annabel related after Heiko came out of his coma, "I think Michael had something to do with saving Heiko. He is our angel now."

On Easter, everyone Michael had touched had come to view this holiday in a different light. Michael, after all, appeared to have brought evidence that there *was* a dimension beyond our five senses, and that he could keep the channels open.

Ludwig and Annabel were discussing how much their life had changed as they drove back from mass that Easter Sunday. They were in a good mood. Heiko had survived his car crash and was recuperating, and Michael's spirit seemed alive to them.

It was Annabel who wondered who was calling that morning as she heard the phone through the front door of their home.

"Ludwig, someone rings the phone," she said. "Quick, then, with the key." Ludwig fumbled for a moment to check his pockets.

As they both stood there, however, they realized that the ringing that issued forth from inside the home was a continuous one, more like a beep, and not an intermittent ring. Both realized at once—but could it be?

Nervously fitting the key into the lock, Ludwig turned the knob and pushed the door open quickly. The sound was more precious than any a heavenly choir could conjure up at that moment.

It was Michael's alarm clock, and it was going off at full volume. It was not broken, nor was it set to go off.

They stood before it, tears in their eyes.

Their boy had come home at last. Even better, Michael was just warming up.

Chapter Fourteen

The Wizard of Reseda

"Now and then two people will make a pact that the one who dies first will make every effort to communicate from the other side and they will agree on a code word or message between them which will identify the communicator and prove his survival of death."

—Leslie Flint, *Voices in the Dark*

March 11, 1997

By now, I was curious to consult professional mediums to see if they could replicate my experiences with mediumship with the spirit of Michael Keller. I was seeking confirmation through other mediums that Michael could communicate specific facts that would provide further evidence that he had survived death.

The ADCs we had experienced provided tantalizing anecdotes, but did not constitute empirical evidence of Michael's continued existence in some afterlife form. I now sought to put Michael to the test—could he repeat the communication phenomenon via informal mediumship experiments?

Jose Vallin, a set designer in Hollywood, upon hearing

of my ADC experiences, suggested that I see a British medium named Brian Hurst, of Resida, California, in order to make further contact with Michael. A professional medium for over 40 years, Hurst holds a B.A. from the University of London. He trained with some of Britain's leading personalities in the field of mediumship and psychic research.

Vallin told me, "Imagine that it's like having a conversation with whoever passed into spirit, and that person is in the next room. Brian Hurst just sits there and listens for the message, then forwards these messages to you. It's nothing more than a three-way conversation. He brings specific facts, specific details, and he does this all with his mind."

I was intrigued.

My friend went on to say that Hurst was a mentor and teacher to James Van Praagh. Like Van Praagh, Hurst had also appeared on television, including the TV shows "The Other Side," "Hard Copy," and the A & E documentary "Beyond Death."

I had been advised to watch out for mediums who engaged in "cold reading," a technique in which the medium takes advantage of a sitter's inclination to find more meaning in a situation than there actually is, and by acting confident and finessing information from a sitter, convinces the sitter he or she is in contact with the spirit world. In a series of guesses, there are "hits" and "misses;" a good cold reader knows that most sitters will forget the "misses" and only remember the "hits."

As a therapist, I decided to approach mediums as a *tabula rasa,* or blank slate. I would not feed them information, but rather would withhold necessary details to see if Michael could spontaneously communicate.

For several days prior to meeting Brian Hurst, I paused from time to time and mentally sent Michael the thought, "If you can communicate with Hurst, name the street where you lived in Germany. Name the Toengesgasse. That will be our code. Toengesgasse."

How could Hurst come up with such a thing at random? It would be difficult to read from my thoughts, via ESP or what is known as "super psi."

"Michael—start by naming the Toengesgasse, and then say whatever you can," I thought, and I repeated the idea several times before the trip to Reseda, California. I knew it might be a long shot for the medium, but nothing for Michael, whose willingness to participate seemed apparent by now.

On the first Saturday in March 1997, I headed for the group reading at Hurst's home. My thoughts were racing, and I was full of questions.

After paying the twelve-dollar entrance fee, I entered Hurst's home for the group reading. Hurst appeared in his slightly cramped living room. A tall, distinguished man with blond hair and extremely blue eyes, Hurst made his entrance from a back room while the crowd buzzed with expectation. A humble man, he made his strong presence felt through silence, smiling until the crowd took notice, and after a series of hushes, began his welcome speech.

"Good evening! Welcome to another night where we will attempt to contact loved ones who have passed into spirit. I'm Brian Hurst, I'm a medium, though the kind of work that I do takes place in the light of day, and not, as you can see, in the dark room of a séance."

Thank God for that, I thought.

"No, my work takes place right here in front of you,

here in the living room of my home. Of course, I have been to séances, and, at one time, I was fortunate enough, back in England, to have had the privilege of sitting with the great medium, Leslie Flint. Flint did conduct his work in a complete black-out, and what wondrous and extraordinary things we witnessed, we who sat with him. Flint has passed into spirit himself, but he has left a legacy in the form of his book, *Voices in the Dark*."

Hurst held the book up and handed it to a young lady seated to his right.

"You see, Flint was best known for a rarity known as Independent Voice Phenomena (IVP). With this phenomena, the voices of spirits, recognizable in many cases to sitters as family and friends alike who have physically died, actually spoke in mid-air."

I couldn't believe what I was hearing. Spirit voices in the air?

"Scientists and skeptics alike came to Flint's sittings, where Leslie allowed investigators and skeptics to put his credibility to the test by putting dye into his mouth, taping it shut with duct tape, having his hands tied to the chair and so forth . . . all to make sure that there was no possible way for him to conduct any type of fraud. Still, the voices came, despite these measures. The British Society for Psychical Research found no fraud whatever. Flint was one of the most tested mediums in this century."

I pictured the lengths that people were willing to go to prove Flint's authenticity, and chuckled at the absurdity of it.

"Tonight, we are going to hear a tape from one of Leslie Flint's sittings."

I braced myself—a tape recording of a dead person? Hurst elaborated:

"When we die, we leave our physical bodies. In a sense, when we are here on Earth, we are like zombies, electrical energy inhabiting a physical shell, but upon death, we shed that shell and the great creative source we call God actually reads that energy like an electronic disk inserted into a vast, spiritual computer."

The 90s metaphor seemed to galvanize attention as Hurst loaded the tape deck.

"When you make it over to the next dimension, you take the form of what you looked like in the prime of your life. You don't have to look old. And now, I'm going to play for you a tape of a spirit named Rose whose independent voice phenomenon was recorded to testify to the fact that death is not the end."

Hurst pressed the play button on his tape deck. Suddenly, the voice of what sounded like an older British woman came from his speakers and instructed on the wonders of the afterlife.

Could this be the real thing? The recorded voice of a disembodied spirit? I couldn't believe it. It had to be a hoax. How could someone make a taped recording of the voice of someone who doesn't have a human body? I remained skeptical.

Now Hurst advised us to prepare for communication with the spirits.

"First, I like to play a piece which kind of loosens things up, and creates a harmonious atmosphere. You see, successful mediumship is aided if you are relaxed, with both feet on the floor. I play this piece called *Swing Wide the Gates of Paradise*, written by Ivor Novello, and to some of you it may seem a bit hokey, but it seems to fit the bill and get things going."

The spectators in his living room reserved judgment and sat still while the recording started. The song sounded exactly like a Jeannette McDonald and Nelson Eddy duet.

This experience was getting more unbelievable by the moment.

Inexplicably, Hurst was drawn straight for me after the tape concluded, and now stood before me with a bright expression on his face.

"George, there's someone here named Bob, or Robert, who wants to speak with you. Do you know anyone named Bob or Robert?"

I knew plenty of Bobs and Roberts. I searched my mind to think of one who had died while Hurst proceeded. I just shrugged, maintaining my *tabula rasa* approach as a sitter.

"George, I'm being told that your father is in spirit."

"Yes," I answered. This was correct.

"I say this because this man says he's your father. Was your father's name Robert?"

"Yes."

"He says he's from Pittsburgh."

Born in 1918 in Pittsburgh, my father had spent all but his last fifteen years living in Highland Park, and then Aspinwall, suburbs of Pittsburgh.

"Yes," I confirmed.

"He says he had problems with his legs before he passed. He's telling me it was down here." Hurst reached down to his shins and calves and brushed them with his hands.

He was right. "Yes." Right before he died, my father had gout from the knees down. In fact, near the end, he couldn't wear his shoes because the gout was so bad and his feet swelled up.

"Yes, he says he was a bit of a mess in this life. He liked to drink a bit, did he?" Again, I was shocked. Group members laughed out loud at the expression on my face.

"He was an alcoholic. He died from cirrhosis of the liver."

"Well, he says he's here now. He says he's very impressed with you. He says, 'You're more of a gentleman than I was.' And he says he's impressed that you've worked with some famous people. He gives me the name—I don't know who this would be . . . he says, James Brown. Who is James Brown?"

At this, I was thoroughly convinced that something extraordinary was happening. In November of 1987, I appeared in a supporting role in the television program *Miami Vice* in an episode entitled "Missing Hours," in a scene with singer James Brown. It was an extremely brief speaking role, and it was highly unlikely that Hurst could have remembered this ten years later. In addition to shooting some TV commercials, I had dabbled in television in the 1980s, though none of the participants at this group demonstration were aware of this.

"Yes, but my father was dead when I worked with James Brown."

"He knows about it now, though. He says he's not going to stop giving messages until you are one hundred percent sure that it's him. He says for me to tell you, 'I'm glad you've gotten over the motorbike bug.' He keeps saying that, the 'Motorbike Bug.'"

"Yes. I used to get into trouble riding motorbikes and nearly had an accident!" I exclaimed.

In 1975, the year my father died, I was nearly killed in a motorbike accident—not motorcycle, motor*bike*. I was thirteen years old. It was one of the last events my father and I shared prior to his passing.

Hurst continued.

"It seems that after your father made the transition into the next dimension, he joined a men's social club, and he tells me that they return to Earth and help spirits make the transition when they die from drink, in places like New York, he tells me. When they die destitute on the street, this group helps them make it across."

How could Hurst have possibly known so many facts about my father's and my relationship? One thing that's nearly impossible to describe is how a keen sense of my father's personality seemed to come through with all of these messages. To bring forth specific facts was one thing, but Hurst's ability to describe his personality was spot-on.

It was, as my friend had foretold, much like a three-way conversation with my dad.

"What about Michael?" I asked, figuring I would strike while the iron was hot.

"Would this be someone younger than you?" Hurst asked.

"Yes," I said.

"I'm getting someone who was very depressed right before he died."

"Yes," I answered, feeling the full spectrum of Hurst's X-ray vision on me.

"Did this man like to go to discotheques and stay up all night long?"

Oh, boy, I thought.

"Yes." I tried to keep a poker face.

"He liked to travel. Did he pass recently?"

"Yes, less than a year ago," I responded.

"Because, sometimes it's difficult for them to get through at first. Often, it takes six months to a year after the death until they've made the adjustment so that they are able to return to this heavy atmosphere and communicate with the living. Wait a minute."

He paused, and closed his eyes.

"It's a very weak signal. He comes through in the tiniest whisper. He says something like, Gas? Gass?"

At first, it didn't register, just gobbledygook from the hereafter. Hurst then put the emphasis on the latter syllable: "Gassé, Gassé." I nearly stood up, and thunder shook my soul.

"Toengesgasse!" I acknowledged. He'd named the street where he lived.

The code had worked.

Chapter Fifteen

The Scole Experimental Group

HOR.   O day and night, but this is wondrous strange!
HAM.   And therefore as a stranger give it welcome.
There are more things in Heaven and Earth, Horatio, than are
dreamt of in your philosophy.

—William Shakespeare, *Hamlet*

April 7, 1997

I called Ludwig and Annabel to break the news that Michael had indeed appeared able to communicate through the medium, Brian Hurst. They were excited.

I explained how, before meeting with Hurst, I had endeavored to create a code by which Michael could communicate that he had made contact with Hurst, and that Hurst had successfully named part of the street where Michael lived, even though he knew nothing of Michael, and had never been to Germany in his life.

I also explained how Hurst facilitated the first conversation that I'd had with my father in twenty-two years, how all of the details had been evidential, and that he had given proper names and accurately related events one after another that had taken place two decades before.

Both Ludwig and Annabel were so taken with the prospect of being able to communicate with Michael via Hurst that they resolved to come to America to see him someday.

As I ended the conversation with Annabel, I could tell that despite the comfort brought by Michael's message to Hurst, the news brought only temporary relief. Michael had been in Los Angeles and sent a message. Now what?

I was delighted, a week after our first meeting, when Brian Hurst invited me to attend one of the "Touched By Angels" seminars with The Scole Experimental Group of Norfolk, England.[5]

When Hurst wrote "Touched By Angels," he meant it literally.

His letter read:

As many of you may already know, I am hosting four of the most famous physical mediums from England at my home and these highly talented people will be conducting lectures and dark-room séances showing physical proof of survival after death.

These meetings are obviously not for beginners or for those of a nervous disposition as the spirit communicators may, at your request, touch you during the course of the séance. I have already sat with these amazing mediums and can vouch for the beauty, benevolence, and authenticity of the phenomena and the reality of its physical nature.

Hurst went on to talk about his own experience with the Scole Group while visiting their experimental site in Norfolk, England:

It is quite obvious that there is no fraud whatever involved in these marvelous displays of spiritual energy. The spirit lights, a hundred times brighter than fireflies, performed gyrations, dances and circles above my head. I was definitely touched a number of times by invisible hands and the supreme experience was the materialization of the gray ghostly hand that stroked my own left palm with its damp, solid reality.

A gray hand materialized and touched him? Was I ready for something like this?

I called Hurst to confirm that I planned to attend. I trusted that the experience was worth investigating.

"George, just to let you know," Hurst forewarned me on the phone, "The Scole Group are physical mediums and don't usually bring personal messages from spirit. It's uncommon, but I think you'll be amazed at the physical phenomena they produce."

Hurst is a kind and honest man. He sees the potential value in investigation of psychic phenomena, and the healing power of evidential after-death communications.

I told him that I was satisfied with the reading he had given me weeks before and wasn't seeking personal communication. I was curious. It was, however, another chance to test the hypothesis that spirit survives death, and the possibility remained that Michael could attempt communication through the Scole Group.

On April 7, 1997, I arrived at Hurst's residence at 6 P.M. Most of the crowd of more than twenty were just pulling up, and so I took advantage of my early arrival to introduce myself to the four members of the Scole Experimental Group.

Robin Foy was a sturdy, large man with an impish grin who could be a younger version of Santa Claus *sans* white beard and moustache. His wife, Sandra, graciously introduced herself, and the other couple in the Scole Group, Diana and Alan Bennett, were attractive and appeared kind. They greeted me as I made my way into Hurst's living room, the place where just weeks before, Hurst had become the sixth person to appear to make contact with Michael.

Robin Foy became interested in physical psychic phenomena in the mid-1970s. Not content with messages passed through mediumistic talents, Foy wanted to see proof of life after death.

In his 1996 book, *In Pursuit of Physical Mediumship*, Robin Foy clarified:

Physical phenomena is very rare in the world today and falls into the category of objective phenomena; that is to say, it is to all intents and purposes based on reality—everybody present is able to see, hear, and feel such manifestations as they occur, and the phenomena itself can be recorded on audio tape or photographed under favorable conditions for posterity, thus proving that the experience is not the result of an over-active imagination.

After a group of roughly twenty-five people had gathered and taken a seat in Hurst's living room, a pre-session lecture commenced.

Robin Foy explained, "The Scole Group's purpose is to produce physical phenomena through mediumship for large groups of people in order to demonstrate survival of bodily death and the existence of a dimension beyond the third dimension."

"The Scole Group," he continued, "have categorized and witnessed one hundred-fifty different types of phenomena, including apports, which are demonstrations of physical objects that appear out of nowhere, brought from individuals from the dimension we call heaven. Also, we have witnessed the opposite, asports, in which objects placed in plain sight have disappeared, having been removed by spirit."

I was astounded. Ulla's earring at Liebrauenberg. Angelina's missing cosmetics. Was it Michael's doing after all?

Foy explained that representatives from NASA and Stanford University had investigated and sat in on Scole experimental sessions, and that scientists and skeptics alike had witnessed the physical phenomena taking place at weekly sittings at the Street Farmhouse in Scole, Norfolk, England.[6]

I found out later that James Van Praagh had sat in on one of these sessions several nights prior to this night, and he later vouched for the authenticity of the experience.

As Foy's lecture concluded, we were asked to remove any watches that had alarms, pagers, anything that would illuminate in the pitch-black darkness and interfere with the session. We were also instructed to leave behind anything that might tingle or chime or ring or give off any sound which could be misconstrued as communication from "the beyond."

Stomach rumbling and palms sweating, I made the short trip into Hurst's garage area, which had been completely blacked out for the occasion. I'd never done anything like this before in my life, and I was mildly anxious.

The seats were placed in a circle, and in the center of the room lay a table with a glass dome on it surrounded by large quartz crystal clusters. Glow-in-the-dark tape marked the four corners of the table. From the rafters above were suspended two pairs of wind chimes, each marked with fluorescent paint. After we were assembled and seated in a large circle, the black-out began.

The Scole Group were easily identified in the dark by virtue of four pairs of glow-in-the-dark wristbands and ankle bracelets which they wore to prove that they remained seated throughout the experiment. Robin Foy, the leader of the group, said a very simple prayer, asking a higher power to allow us all to witness an experiment of physical phenomena. There were some "Amens," and then one of the group began to play classical music on a portable cassette tape deck.

At first, I thought, what if nothing happens? How could they guarantee phenomena? I'd never heard of such a thing.

Foy had explained that they conducted experimental sessions twice weekly in Norfolk and that they have developed a relationship with a "spirit team" of scientists in the next dimension that is committed to show up and facilitate phenomena.

A few minutes passed in total darkness.

The first thing I noticed was an enormous cold breeze blow past me. Hurst was taping the session, and participants were invited to call out whenever they experienced anything out of the ordinary.

"I feel a huge cold breeze!" a participant offered.

Others piped up, having experienced the breeze at the same time on the opposite end of the room.

"Oh, I'm being touched!" a woman called out. "Someone just reached out and caressed the top of my hand!" She asked those around her if anyone else was responsible. A chorus of *no*s indicated the likely cause as being a materialized spirit. "I felt the hand, the contour of the hand!" she exclaimed.

Foy explained, "The spirits actually have the power to materialize in a form very similar to their earthly body. If you are frightened, they will not disturb you, so you mustn't worry."

Another participant, Tricia Loar of Glendale, California, exclaimed, "I'm holding someone's hand. They're shaking my hand, and I can feel clothes on this spirit's arm, like drapery!"

"What is it?" Foy called out.

"I felt up the arm and . . ."

"Yes?"

"There's no body above the shoulder!"

I later found out that Tricia held a masters degree in English, had taught English for more than fifteen years before operating a small business in Los Feliz, California. Neither skeptic nor zealous believer, Loar was impressed by the sitting.

Suddenly, out of nowhere, a light formed in front of me on the floor, traveling to within inches of my feet, then quickly ascended to the ceiling, disappearing into the rafters.

Moments later, another light appeared on the table in the center of the room. I leaned forward to get a better look; this was unbelievable. Were these the same kind of lights that Heiko Keller had experienced back in June of 1996, I wondered? Tiny spheres about the size of a pea, some of the lights varied in size and appeared as big around as marbles.

The lights appeared like sparks, and did not appear to be the result of any projection of light or laser nor were they produced by fiber optics. If one cupped these light spheres in one's hand (and some did), they would glow like a firefly, though they were definitely *not* fireflies.

Since Michael appeared able to receive my thoughts in this same "other dimension," I resolved to conduct a private experiment as I sat witnessing this.

I sent the message out in my mind, "If anyone can hear this, I'm putting both of my hands out in the dark in front of me. If you can hear me, I want you to send one of the lights to touch my *right* hand. Send a light to the *right* hand."

A moment later, a light zoomed from out of nowhere, headed straight for me, and touched the index finger of my right hand!

I couldn't believe it. It felt like a solid object. Solid light?

Just then, another light formed on the table in the center of the room, and I noticed it went down onto the floor through the table! Hurst called out, "Did you see that? The light went through a solid object—it landed on the top of the table, went through it, and now it is on the floor."

People continued to call out that they had been touched, some people saying they could feel the contour of the hand touching them, count the fingers, or feel the warmth. All the while, the Scole Team remained seated, visible via their glow-in-the-dark bracelets.

From out of nowhere, unseen forces set off one pair of wind chimes that Brian Hurst and the Scole Group had suspended from a beam running across the center of the ceiling of the garage. Soon afterward, the group witnessed an unseen force hoisting up the fluorescent base of the chimes, which lifted to the ceiling, and remained there for several minutes.

It was at this point that medium Diana Bennett singled me out in the group. I am including the verbatim account from the Scole Session:

BENNETT: George: do you know someone in spirit? It's a man, just a minute. Well, they are saying, thanks for the thoughts you are sending out for people (like him). Hard for this person.

GEORGE: Is the person communicating through you, coming to me?

BENNETT: He's coming closer. Do you act?

GEORGE: Yes, I do.

BENNETT: Commercials, is that what you call them here?

GEORGE: Yes. I have a commercial running, that's right.

BENNETT: He's talking about it you see. Because he's distant, he's having a bit of a battle.

GEORGE: I understand what he's saying. I understand what he's trying to communicate with you; he knows I do commercials.

BENNETT: Just a minute . . . he did drugs he says.

GEORGE: Yes, yes.

BENNETT: Yes, I feel you are connected well with this man. It's not easy to bring him nearer under these circumstances.

GEORGE: That's O.K.

BENNETT: But you know, your thoughts helped him; you sent out prayers for him at the time. And they were well received and helped him because he was very confused, that's the word.

GEORGE: Thank you so much.

BENNETT: Not lost, that's not the word, but confused. It's been a long adjustment to get to this level. Where he is now. But he is progressing slowly and learning a lot more. He links with you because, he says, you are going to have a break that he didn't get. Don't know what he means, but you can think about it when you're on your own, perhaps.

GEORGE: Does he have anything to say to his parents?

BENNETT: Well, he's sorry, of course, because he sees things differently now. Things were all out of balance and out of proportion. The drugs he was taking heightened the mood, then it just tipped the balance of things.

GEORGE: Yes, anything specific for the parents?

BENNETT: Don't bother with the grave so much.

GEORGE: Tell him I understand.

BENNETT: I just wanted to connect you in, because he's been waiting patiently, a long while.

GEORGE: Is he in the room?

BENNETT: Oh, yes, but he's not a good communicator, not with this energy, I would say, when there are so many souls here tonight.

GEORGE: Yes, I understand.

BENNETT: Well do give his "folks," he says, his love. Do give it a miss (a rest), that old grave. He's not there, of course. He's moved on. They can link with his memory in a nicer way than that. There are a lot of tears every time they go, and that's not helping. Not helping them go forward or him, really.

GEORGE: Thank you.

The session had lasted two hours, and by the time it finished, I felt I was in shock.

I didn't ask Ms. Bennett to attempt to contact Michael. I had never met her before in my life. Neither Ms. Bennett nor Hurst knew that I have worked as a commercial actor. In fact, I had introduced myself to Hurst as a social worker, when we met several weeks back. Only Michael knew me as a commercial actor. I shot several commercials prior to finishing my masters degree in Florida while Michael was visiting me.

Hurst had not informed Diana Bennett of any information regarding Michael. Indeed, I deliberately withheld details regarding myself and Michael's passing when I met Hurst in March.

It's important to note that Diana Bennett brought information from Michael that Hurst didn't know. For instance, neither Bennett nor Hurst had known that Michael's parents were visiting Michael's grave several times per day, nor had either one known that I had offered prayers, at the time Michael died, at the garden sanctuary of a nearby church.

Also, how could Ms. Bennett have known that drugs had been discovered in Michael's system after the accident? It appeared to be Michael's way of communicating in a way that left no doubt whatsoever that it was he. Chance didn't explain the accuracy of these messages.

How could she be familiar with the mysterious circumstances surrounding his death, details Hurst had no knowledge of? Furthermore, Ms. Bennett had accurately described the scene, saying via Michael that "things were all out of balance and out of proportion. The drugs he was taking heightened the mood, then it just tipped the balance of things."

After the meeting concluded, I reflected that by making contact via the Scole Group, Michael appeared to have communicated with or through *seven* people to date, including (1) Heiko Keller, (2) myself, (3) Ulla Simic, (4 & 5) Ludwig and Annabel Keller, (6) Brian Hurst, and (7) Diana Bennett.

Who would be number eight, I wondered.

Chapter Sixteen

A New World

"I can now turn and see how far I've come, and look forward to the distances I have left to travel."

—John Edward, *Crossing Over*

When I left Hurst's home after the Scole Experiment, it was a new world that greeted me as I got into my car to return to Hollywood.

It appeared that I had seen and heard things that most people have only glanced at as fictions in movies or on TV. I was less skeptical of the authenticity of the Scole Group after they appeared to bring Michael through spontaneously with such specific information. The "spirit light" that touched my hand seems no less a miracle to me now as you read this than at the moment when the event occurred.

I began a written correspondence with Diana Bennett, and she wrote to encourage me to continue working on this book. In one letter, she advised: "Remember, all this phenomena is possible by the power of love and is directed by evolved beings."

I was cautious with whom I discussed the Scole Experiment, because some might associate The Scole Group's work as being about witchcraft or magic or fraud, instead of being a scientific experiment to test the hypothesis of the survival of human spirit after physical death.[7]

I related the information to Ludwig and Annabel and shared the amazement at Michael's miraculous seventh contact, which further eased their bereavement.

"He says, 'Don't visit the grave so much.' I think he worries that you don't believe he's O.K., and that's why he does all these things." I firmly believed this by now.

"I understand," Ludwig said, resigned but jubilant. He accepted this communication from his son, moving closer to acceptance of his son's destiny.

In May of 1997, I received a letter from Leland H. Roloff, Ph. D., of the C. G. Jung Institute of Chicago. He was a Jungian analyst and friend whom I had asked for feedback regarding the messages. He wrote:

"You have to understand that it (Michael's spirit) might very well be seeking some kind of power over every one of you. My take is that the spirit has not been suitably interred or given over to its new destiny."

Dr. Roloff acknowledged the possibility of the phenomenon, but expressed suspicion regarding the motive behind it. Why was Michael's spirit being so persistent, he seemed to be asking.

I couldn't blame Dr. Roloff for worrying about our welfare. I was grateful that he listened, took our experiences at face value, and didn't write off the ADCs and mediumship as a bereavement hallucination or the product of wishful thinking and overactive imaginations.

I returned to Reseda for an individual session with Brian Hurst, and he brought more messages from Michael.

"Write the book, write it!" he said.

"I didn't tell you I'm writing a book," I said.

"Well, that's what Michael says. Also, Michael gives a hello to Ursula. Please say 'thanks to Ursula.'" Hurst insisted.

I didn't know anyone by that name. As I'd been told, with mediumship there are "hits," and there are "misses."

"Brian, I'll check later on that one." I said.

"And Ina, Ina—Ina would be someone alive, on Earth, in Germany?"

Ina Tharandt was a colleague and one of Michael's best friends for years in Germany, though I had never met her. How on Earth could Hurst pick up a name like "Ina"?

"Yes, Brian." Bull's-eye!

"Michael says she has a problem with the nose." He was confident that Michael was communicating this. "Yes, check with her. I see Michael holding his hands over his nose like something is wrong."

I tracked down Ina Tharandt in Frankfurt, and we had a long discussion on the phone. She remained sad over Michael's loss, and stated that she had distanced herself from him the last two months of his life, when things seemed to go out of control.

I turned the conversation toward Hurst's revelation, holding my breath.

"Ina, this is a strange question—but have you had any problem with your nose recently, a cold, perhaps?"

"Funny you should ask," she said. "I've had allergies for the last three weeks, I've been sneezing out of the blue, and I've never had allergies. How did you know that?"

I explained about Hurst, and about my writing *Messages*.

After the conversation, Ina never called me again.

Later, when I mentioned the messages brought through Brian Hurst to Thorsten Jacques on the phone, I discovered that "Ulla" is a nickname for Ursula. "She is Ursula Simic, but we just call her Ulla," Thorsten declared.

I was at a party in May 1997 when I suddenly became ill at ease.

"He's in the hospital." The voice was back.

"I know he's still in the hospital, Michael," I thought, for Michael's brother Heiko had sustained devastating injuries to both his legs in his auto crash, and his recuperation was projected to take six months to a year.

I nodded to friends, continuing conversing with them while my fight-or-flight system kicked into a state of alarm. I didn't question the voice, I went home. I knew that something was wrong.

I discovered Annabel's voice on the answering machine. She was crying.

"I hate to call you . . . with this . . . but . . . Ludwig has . . . had . . . a . . . stroke! He's in . . . the hospital."

It turned out to be bad, and Ludwig's prospects for survival were poor. The next evening brought another ADC: I brought a load of laundry from the basement to my apartment and went to my bedroom to sort my clothes. After ten minutes, I walked back into the living room, when I noticed that my front door was being held wide open by unseen hands.

No one was there.

The door wasn't stuck, and it wasn't the wind. I'd never seen anything like this before in my life. I had to reach over, and physically close the door. I got the message, of course, and I called Germany.

Ralph Keller, Michael's eldest brother, answered and solemnly reported the latest on Ludwig: "The doctors say he's going to die," Ralph told me. "Or worse, he could become a vegetable."

Chapter Seventeen

Happy Anniversary

"She—whose name starts off like an endearment and ends like a crack of the whip. Marlene . . . Dietrich!"

—Jean Cocteau, quoted in *Marlene*
by Marlene Dietrich

A year had passed, and no one had come forward to explain what happened to Michael that day, June 10, 1996. The women who hit him never regained their memory of that night, though both drivers made a full recovery in every other aspect.

Ludwig survived, but remained gravely ill for weeks, and it was a terrible time for Annabel. At first, doctors informed her that he would be an invalid, conveying a negative outlook for his recovery. Still, he inched along, and surprised all of us when he began to talk on the phone within a month. He seemed to defy the odds as he struggled to get better, though he remained at a hospital in Bad Neustadt; nearly a three-hour drive from the Keller home in Kirschfurt.

Heiko remained in a hospital at Dresden, a victim of an

infection he contracted after months of recuperation. He was told that after the infection passed, he would have to start his recovery from scratch. By June, he had undergone five operations on his feet and legs to undo the trauma he suffered in February, and more operations were imminent.

I worried for Annabel because she would be alone on the anniversary of Michael's death. Ludwig's stroke threatened to send her into depression, as she had little support and complained frequently of insomnia, fatigue, and feelings of hopelessness in light of the many crises she had suffered. Michael's eldest brother, Ralph, worked nearby on the Keller estate, but had a family of his own to go home to at night. He could support his mother during the day, but Annabel would face the nights alone.

Annabel had become like a mother to me, and without a support base, I feared that she might fall into a major depression, and I was determined to do everything in my power to prevent it.

Mail arrived in the States on the anniversary of Michael's death on the 10th, including my first copy of The Scole Experimental Group's magazine, *The Spiritual Scientist*.

I had sent The Scole Group a photo of Michael to put a face on the identity of the contact made during the demonstration of the Group at Brian Hurst's home in April. I also explained that it appeared that Diana Bennett had become the seventh person to have contact with the discarnate spirit of Michael.

I opened the magazine to discover a reference to Michael's communication during the Scole Experiment:

"Since his passing in June 1996, Michael K. has been determined to prove his continued existence and has communicated to his friend, his parents, a brother, a work colleague, Brian Hurst (a British medium residing in California), and finally through the Scole Group."

Michael's messages were now in print. I glanced at Michael's picture, now glaring at me confidently as if to say, "I did it!"

He had made the headlines on Earth from heaven.

Alarm clock ADCs marked the anniversary of Michael's physical death. Three, in fact.

Mine, on June 7, 1997, in the United States, was placed on the middle of my bed again while I was out. This time, I called a neighbor upstairs and asked him to photograph it.

At the Keller home in Germany, two alarm clocks went off on the anniversary of Michael's accident: the alarm in Annabel's bedroom and Michael's personal alarm clock. One of them continued to go on and off for more than a week. Neither clock was broken or set to go on. At one point, both alarm clocks were going off at the same time. Annabel was not alone in the house after all.

Annabel called, and afterwards I preserved the answering machine tape, which featured her holding the receiver to one alarm clock, and crying out: "Do you hear it? Do you hear it?"

I'd come full circle a year later, and I was seeking closure on these experiences. I had repeatedly attempted to arrange an individual sitting with James Van Praagh. This was prior to the publication of *Talking to Heaven: A Medium's Message of Life After Death*, which quickly rose to number one on *The New York Times* bestseller list in March 1998 and catapulted Van Praagh to fame and fortune.

I saw an opportunity for Van Praagh to reach even more people and to allow his abilities to be challenged in a test—to bring Michael Keller through yet one more time.

Van Praagh, I was told by a personal assistant, was too busy and was no longer giving private readings. His television appearances alone created a grueling schedule, and he later explained to me that his office received up to 5000 letters per week.

It turned out to be a fortuitous twist of fate.

Through a referral from Van Praagh's personal assistant, Cammy Farone, I attended a May 30, 1997, group demonstration he headed up at The Sportsmen's Lodge in Studio City. It was there I was introduced to another extraordinary medium from England—Robert Brown.

It was an impressive demonstration, though few people get to make contact in such large groups. The event was attended by over a thousand people, evidence of the growing popularity of the phenomenon of mediumship.

Van Praagh was more riveting to watch live than on television. That night he only "read" a few sitters, but the emotional connection he established with people and the messages he received appeared so specific that people were amazed.

Of course, people attending such events may want to believe so much that they can communicate with deceased loved ones that they will find no fault in the medium and adore the "hits" and ignore the "misses."

I made a point of interviewing several of the people that Van Praagh and Brown "read," during one of the breaks, and discovered to my satisfaction that they did not appear to have been planted in the audience. I asked them if he had correctly identified names and relationships of people who had passed into spirit, and the respondents identified exactly who had been contacted, what dates and evidential information had been accurate. Some even produced photographs and letters from loved ones who had passed, as evidence of a successful reading.

Robert Brown held his ground with Van Praagh, producing startling details through his mediumship for grateful, and often tearful, audience members.

Afterwards, I turned my attention to Brown. I discovered he was giving private readings in California before returning to Britain and then traveling to Munich.

I called and made an appointment. I then called Annabel in Germany.

An idea had occurred to me: what about having Mrs. Keller send a message *by thought* to Michael's spirit, and then having Michael relay the message to Brown in Los Angeles?

I could then act as a "proxy sitter," sitting on behalf of a third party about whom the medium would know nothing. If evidential communications could manifest through Brown, especially a coded message, the explanation couldn't be explained by telepathy with the persons present, or by chance or coincidence. In other words, Brown couldn't read something that wasn't *in my mind* in the first place.

It seemed like an interesting experiment. If successful, this experience promised to be a kind of final proof for Annabel of Michael's survival.

When we spoke, I proposed the idea, and asked her to create a code, something known only to her, to see if we could replicate my experiences with Hurst and Bennett and prove, once and for all, that her communication with Michael could continue, perhaps indefinitely.

I saw this as an opportunity for her to move from depression to acceptance of Michael's new state of being. If she came to see that he was still accessible to her, perhaps this would redefine the loss in a new way.

"I will create a code of my own," she said. "Only Michael will know what that is, and I wish you luck with this man." Annabel seemed confident.

Her incredible love for her son, and her open-mindedness, impressed me. Could Michael deliver another coded message, we wondered. A message sent from Germany to the heavens and then to Los Angeles?

In late June, I arrived at noon for a half-hour individual session with Robert Brown at the Walter Dunn Foundation in Anaheim.

Born in London, Brown is a noted lecturer, teacher, and minister of the Christian Spiritualist Society. A contemporary of Van Praagh, Brown serves various churches throughout Europe and shares his gift with support groups for families grieving the loss of a child. Brown also bears the distinction of having given mediumistic sittings for members of the British Royal Family, including the late Princess Diana; the Gandhi family; and singer Elton John.

Brown also gave mediumistic readings for the late Marlene Dietrich on several occasions at her apartment in Paris. I found in this the greatest irony, considering that I had met Michael Keller over a book on Marlene Dietrich, and, now, I was consulting her medium to talk with Michael again!

A skeptic turned reluctant believer, Dietrich had told Brown, "If anybody asks me, I will say I don't believe in life after death, even though I do."

After a brief introduction, I sat down with Brown, and

told him nothing about why I'd come to see him. Neither Hurst nor Van Praagh were aware I was consulting with Brown, and neither had an opportunity to pass along information regarding Michael or his death.

As I sat before Brown, I again became a blank slate, withholding information and replying "yes"/ "no" during the session. Clearly Brown could not have engaged in "cold reading," as a verbatim text of our session demonstrates:

GEORGE: Tell me about Michael.

BROWN: I got somebody who passed relatively young. Do you know how he passed?

GEORGE: Yes. Do you want me to tell you?

BROWN: No. I felt to some degree that he was always someone who was doing things rather fast. So, even if you checked up on it, he's someone who learned to walk before the average age, learned to talk before the average age, and this is someone who was trying to cram everything in. And the way he passed . . . did he pass quite fast?

GEORGE: Yes.

BROWN: It all makes sense with the way of passing. I think, not only was this someone who had to learn things, obviously the reason for being here, but I felt that this was someone who brought lessons into other people's lives. Do you know if he knocked his head at all?

GEORGE: Yes.

BROWN: I felt this was fairly fast, and there was this point of almost hovering, of . . . we get a choice of going or not. I felt that if this person had stayed, he would have been totally dependent upon people, and this was quite an independent spirit. But I felt he actually set a lot in motion. Left so many things unfinished, but set a lot in motion, and I got someone who's quite quick with the mind.

GEORGE: Yes.

BROWN: Do you know if there was glass involved when he passed?

GEORGE: Yes, it was an auto crash.

BROWN: It was a crash. But he didn't pass there and then. I got the impression—"I've knocked my head, I'm still aware of people around." But he says that he was around, and I don't know if they tried to revive him at the scene?

GEORGE: Yes, they did.

BROWN: He says, "There was no point." In fact, he says, "There was no point in going to the hospital." The face is quite attractive. I asked him, "Was it your fault?" and he answered, "What does it matter whose fault it was, I'm here now."

BROWN: And I said, "It sounds like you've got regrets," and he said, "No. I started so many things. He'll (George) be able to work with me." And I said, "How's he going to do that?" And he said he's "leading you into meeting people." He's says he's had a hand in guiding you because you keep sending up all these different questions. And, do you keep a photograph of him on display?

GEORGE: Yes.

BROWN: He says you talk a lot to him, and I said, "The photograph?" and he said, "No, he sits and talks to me quite a lot." And, I felt that his parents are not over this.

GEORGE: No, they're not.

BROWN: He's saying something about the mother,

I don't know if you're in contact with her. He says
that she has a watch belonging to him. He says,
"She has my watch." And, also, he wishes that she
would get on with her life because it seems to have
come to a bit of a stop. Now, his mother doesn't
understand all of this, and to some degree is a little
bit afraid.

GEORGE: Yes, that's absolutely true.

BROWN: And, he says that he's been to you in
your dreams. He says that he wants to give you
more information, and tell you more things, and
that's one of the reasons that he found at the
moment to contact you via dreams, because it
seems that when you meditate that you're not
going deep enough.

GEORGE: Could you please ask him, did the car
hit him by accident?

BROWN: He said that he wasn't concentrating.
His mind wasn't very clear; he actually felt sorry
for the other people. Did other people pass as well?

GEORGE: A woman nearly died!

BROWN: He said, "They had to push her back in
the body! They had to push her back in." And he
said, he was sorry if he would have caused that
because it was his own doing, to some degree.

GEORGE: He said that?

BROWN: Yes. He gets on very well with you, and
he seems to want to dictate things to you, and to
some degree, I think it's part of your book.

GEORGE: The book's *about* him. I didn't tell you
that.

BROWN: No. Because he said, "We'll get it right!"
He's interested in dictating more and more.

GEORGE: Am I keeping him from going on?

BROWN: No, you can't do that because, just the same as you have free will to come here today, he has free will. Letting go means accepting the situation, so we can't hold on to anyone. Accepting that life goes on.

GEORGE: I see.

BROWN: I think he's going to be a bit of a character, this friend of yours, because I think he's the kind that, if you were at a physical séance, he could play around.

Brown had no idea that Michael had already "played around" during the Scole Experiment, and unknowingly confirmed my "touched by an angel" experience with the spirit light at the Scole Group sitting, as well as Diana Bennett's mediumistic contact with Michael.

Now came the time for the ultimate test of the credibility of these cumulative experiences.

Had Brown been able to bring a message which would leave no doubt in Annabel Keller's mind that Michael's spirit had survived death and could communicate back to her? Could he "hear" her thoughts, and transmit a code across the Atlantic back to Germany?

I felt that in healing her sadness and loss, it was imperative that Annabel be allowed to demonstrate for herself the powerful interaction with a professional medium, but I had no power over the outcome of the experiment.

Annabel called unexpectedly from Bad Neustadt and I told her about the reading. Of course she had the watch, she had everything he owned, I thought, but still I told her:

"Brown says there's a message for you."

"Yes?" she asked.

"I feel funny about it, Annabel, because it . . . well, it had to do with something that belonged to Michael that you obviously have."

"Go on." She was excited.

"Brown says that Michael says, and I quote: 'She has my watch.'"

"Yes. It's on my arm! That was our code! I said, 'Tell Brown I have the watch.'"

She had worn Michael's Rolex on the trip from Kirschfurt to Bad Neustadt.

I decided to take a trip to Palm Springs to finish documenting these experiences. I felt compelled to tell this story, about how a tragedy gave birth to an informal series of experiments in which I put to test the hypothesis that the human spirit survives death.

There were friends that I had met through Brian Hurst who were very interested in seeing that I finished writing this story. In Germany, the Kellers continued to endorse the telling of our story, with Annabel hoping that it might offer help to other parents who may be grieving the loss of a child.

Thorsten Jacques had been supportive of the completion of *Messages*, though he remained resistant to any *direct* spiritual contact. He feared it would throw him off balance and upset him, though he had been unable to forget the day that fate thrust him into the "driver's seat" to overhear the conversation between Ulla Simic and myself on July 5, 1996, when this journey was just beginning.

Angelina called on the anniversary of Michael's death, explaining that she had experienced ADCs with Michael in Germany, but steadfastly refused to discuss it over the phone. She insisted I fly to Germany to hear about her encounter with Michael's soul, which took place in her apartment.

I also received a call from Ulla. She said the mysterious experiences related to Michael's spirit had ceased and that she had "returned to the land of the living." She told me that she had fallen in love and planned to marry. Her job was safe, and her status at Lufthansa secure.

I was amazed when a colleague at the community mental health center where I work handed me a journal out of the blue: *Philosophy, Psychiatry and Psychology*. He thought I might be interested in an article, "Spiritual Experience and Psychopathology" (vol. 4.1. John Hopkins University Press, 1997).

In it, researchers Mike Jackson, Ph.D., and K.W.M. Fulford, Ph.D., documented that "A recent study of the relationship between spiritual experience and psychopathology suggested that psychotic phenomena could occur in the context of spiritual experiences rather than mental illness."

The article lent credence in the professional mental health community to the existence of ADCs. The writers discovered that some supernatural communications were not only "benign," but potentially therapeutic experiences outside of the context of mental illness.

Jackson and Fulford advocated further research of "strange" spiritual events, such as hearing the voice of a deceased loved one in one's mind, to come to a better understanding of these experiences.

I was packing to leave for Palm Springs, channel surfing with the remote, when Dietrich suddenly appeared on the screen, sitting on a barrel in a clip from *The Blue Angel* singing *Falling in Love Again*.

A fitting send-off, I thought, and a reminder of the day I met Michael Keller. It was a special on Dietrich called *Shadow And Light*, produced by Dietrich's grandson, David Riva. Maria Riva appeared before me in Hollywood, on my big screen offering clarification of the image and the substance of her mother, Marlene Dietrich.

"I think Dietrich's life is a tragedy from beginning to end," she said as clips of Dietrich's recently discovered first screen test in 1929 revealed a rebellious up-and-coming star.

Riva went on to discuss Dietrich's character defects, her narcissism, her alcohol abuse, the excessive life of a Hollywood celebrity.

I thought about how Dietrich helped to popularize image over substance, and I admired her daughter's courage to publicly separate Dietrich's persona from the real person.

I wished Michael Keller had identified with Riva's crusade, because he was a person who was constantly looking for substance, for love, and a place to feel safe. He found safety at home with his parents, and, for a while, with me, but as he grew up and went abroad, he went searching for a new home in a world corroded by the effect of Dietrich's icon, a world awash in image and superficiality. "Protect me from this world," Michael asked me the day I met him. Regrettably, despite my education, my training in social work, and my unconditional love for Michael, his destiny was beyond my control.

I had never been to Palm Springs, and it was therapeutic to see the urban landscape of Los Angeles meld into green peaks, then flat yellows and desert grays, until, finally, I was on a two-lane road in the middle of the desert.

I had packed the Dietrich book by Maria Riva that Michael had given me as a present. Dietrich's eyes on the dust jacket stared back at me hauntingly, but with a strange look of satisfaction. I was not alone on this trip.

As I sped along the narrowing two-lane road into the desolate, arid outskirts of Palm Springs, I accepted that it would be a challenge to write about my spiritual experiences. I accepted that it was a risk, but that others would likely experience messages of their own and need to know it was safe to talk about them. My notebooks piled high, my Dictaphone ready to record, I was determined to finish writing this book. I would tell the truth about the messages from Michael Keller, and how love bridged the gap between this world and the spirit world we call "heaven."

I turned up the CD player, playing *Lola* from the soundtrack of the original picture, *The Blue Angel*. The wind picked up as Dietrich's voice boomed, "Lola! Lola! Everybody knows me! Ask the first person you see, they'll tell you where to find me! Old men, young men, all fall into my net—"

I looked up. Out of nowhere, a lone, huge billboard appeared off to the right:

PALM SPRINGS DINING HOT SPOT

BLUE ANGEL

BAR & GRILLE

Chapter Eighteen

Your Messages

"Let one who seeks not stop seeking until one finds. When one finds, one will be troubled. When one is troubled, one will marvel and will rule over all."

—Jesus Christ from *The Gospel of Thomas*,
translation by Marvin Meyer

It stands to reason that others can replicate experiences, similar to ours, with the spirits of their loved ones.

We all make choices, and we all have free will. This appears to be true of individuals who have passed through the transition we call death, and, so, it is important to remember that it is the strength of the relationship with them that may be an important variable that makes ADC experiences possible.

One could pray and meditate and not make contact, if the person one is attempting to reach doesn't want to communicate or lacks the skill to do so. It may take a certain amount of practice for them—who knows what the variables are?

For those interested in learning how to initiate ADCs, here are some suggestions based upon my experiences:

Ask. After-death communication involves a willingness to send and receive messages. Find a quiet place where you can be alone in your thoughts. Thoughts are like radio signals. They originate from one's self and have a destination. Be open to the possibility of receiving thoughts from departed loved ones as well as sending them.

Close your eyes, and focus your thoughts on the party you are trying to reach. Allow time for the message to be sent and then received. While you wait, pray to higher powers to open the channels of communication. Prayer is speaking to, and meditation, listening.

Send one message at a time, and make your messages specific.

Listen; know what to look for: Become familiar with the many ways that those we love can communicate after they leave this life.

It seems likely that one may be more sensitive to receiving ADCs after a recent loss. Remember, the person you are trying to reach most likely has all the time in the world to get back to you. As long as you are alive, and they have passed from bodily death into the next dimension, they may be accessible for ADCs, mediumship, and phenomena.

Try to listen for the sound of their voices. You will recognize when they communicate because it will sound similar to when you last spoke to them in person or on the phone.

And, learn the difference between your thoughts and a thought which is put into your mind, like a kind of ethereal e-mail from a discarnate loved one.

Some may be unable to distinguish between the creation in one's head of an imaginary voice, and the actual communication. Keep at it. Ask for specific answers when you send your thoughts out; what proof will your loved one need to offer to confirm that it is they who are communicating? What will truly confirm the experience as real?

Think with unconditional love: When thoughts are joined with unconditional love, miracles happen. Being loving while sending thoughts out to the next dimension may be crucial.

It is an obvious fact that it is only a matter of time until each of us is separated from our parents, children, husbands, wives, lovers. Life in this dimension, on this planet, is a finite, temporal experience.

If we can focus our energy in each of our relationships so that the quality of our love strives to be unconditional, we can erase separation in the here and now. Unconditional love may be a bridge that makes it much easier for mediumship and phenomena to take place. I believe it shrinks the distance between the dimensions.

Loving unconditionally means releasing expectations. It means not being possessive of the one you love. It is not so much about achieving perfect love in the here and now, but about choosing to stop judging *anyone* ever again.

Fault-finding, for instance, is the opposite of loving unconditionally. *A Course in Miracles*[8] paraphrases this sentiment, "Would you rather be happy, or would you rather be right?"

Write a note: It may sound ridiculous, but this suggestion, first made to me by medium Brian Hurst, has been the most successful way of getting the attention of a spirit and relaying specific, directed communication. A written note left out in a prominent place is like an e-mail waiting to get picked up in cyberspace. Eventually your loved one will see it, or it will be seen by someone and the news relayed to your loved one. Leave the note on display for at least several weeks.

In this therapeutic forum, you can say anything you want and ask for confirmation that the message was received (electrical phenomena, a coded message through a medium, materialization).

Have patience: Repeating requests via prayer and then listening for messages seems to have been the key to getting results in my experience. The first communication with Michael took place after a week of daily prayer and meditation.

If you haven't personally experienced results in a reasonable time period, investigate the possibility of visiting a professional medium.

In Los Angeles, Robert Brown, Brian Hurst, and Laurie Campbell are professional mediums that make contact for people in individual and group sessions. They can be contacted online at the following URLs:

Robert Brown: http://www.robertbrown-medium.com

Brian Hurst: http://www.ktb.net/~hurani

Laurie Campbell: http://www.lauriecampbell.net

James Van Praagh no longer accepts private appointments, but continues to meet with people in groups: http://www.vanpraagh.com

On the East Coast, I recommend the following mediums:

John Edward: http://www.johnedward.net

George Anderson: http://www.georgeanderson.com

Suzane Northrop: http://www.theseance.com

Be advised that the mediums I've listed have waiting lists and can't guarantee results, though I agree with Gary Schwartz's observation that these are the "Michael Jordans of mediumship."

A more comprehensive listing of mediums can be found at the Guggenheims' ADC Project at: http://www.after-death.com

If it isn't possible to consult the above referenced mediums, I suggest that you check the Yellow Pages in your area for a Spiritualist Church in your area. They may be able to refer you to a credible medium.

Subsequent to the completion of *Messages,* The Scole Experimental Group in Norfolk, England disbanded. Still, they can be accessed on the Internet at http://www.psisci.force9.co.uk.

What if nothing happens? If you don't immediately make contact, it doesn't mean that you have failed, or that your loved ones have turned their backs on you, when they could come back.

It could mean that you or your loved ones aren't ready for the experience yet.

I'm certain that many readers will develop the skill to invite loved ones back into their lives to keep the communication going.

Please remember that it is vital as well to continue to form and build new relationships with the living in the here and now.

Epilogue

Since completing this book, the Kellers have made significant gains, despite losses that threatened to keep them from moving on. Both Annabel and Ludwig went on to have ADC experiences, and Michael appears to watch over them from the vantage point of his latest destination.

My life has prospered in many ways, both professionally and interpersonally. I was approached by people seeking bereavement consultations that included mediumship. I discovered that the gift that started with communications with Michael now extends to others, and I continue to accept referrals as time allows. I have become an advocate of research of mediumship in a controlled lab setting.

Serious research of mediumship is already being carried out at the University of Arizona's Human Energy Systems Laboratory (HESL) under the auspices of Gary E. Schwartz, Ph.D., and Linda G. Russek, Ph.D., as detailed in their collaboration, *The Living Energy Universe* (Hampton Roads, 1999) and featured as the subject of the 1999 HBO special, *Life Afterlife*. Mediums are now being tested, and their accuracy rates recorded, in increasingly more stringent, controlled settings. Dr. Schwartz has set about to discover any data in favor of proving or *disproving* the hypothesis that the human spirit survives physical "death." The motto of the Human Energy Systems Lab is "Let the data speak."

I remain hopeful that research of ADCs and mediumship will expand and that experiments like the ones recently conducted at the University of Arizona will be replicated and extended at other labs.

We owe it to future generations to share the truth that our destiny may include after-death communication, and that no one need suffer unnecessarily painful or lengthy bereavement resulting from the temporary separations that occur at the end of each physical life. That is the gift Michael Keller brought to me, Ulla Simic, Angelina Usai, Annabel and Ludwig Keller, and Heiko Keller, and which potentially he brings to all who read this book.

Subsequent to completing this book, the confirmation I sought through consultations with legitimate mediums, coupled with ADC experiences, turned out to be less singular an experience than I had thought.

Professionals, friends, and associates, reported that they had replicated my experiences. Some reported to me that they documented successful consultations with several professional mediums and that they received evidence repeatedly from the same spirit. Several of these individuals also experienced ADCs, and these experiences were concurrent with evidential consultations with professional mediums.

I look forward to future efforts of researchers who incorporate science and spirituality to work together in greater harmony as we proceed into unexplored domains, regardless of the outcome.

I remain open to the data and discoveries that result from having science put spirit to the test, and remain committed to actively participate as a research subject in the years to come.

Bibliography

I acknowledge the following authors and publishers for the material that I quoted throughout this book:

Buhlman, William. *Adventures Beyond the Body: How to Experience Out-of-Body Travel*. San Francisco: HarperCollins, 1966.

Carroll, Robert Todd. *The Skeptic's Dictionary*. Skepdic.com, 2000.

———*Diagnostic and Statistical Manual of Mental Disorders, Fourth Edition*. Washington, D.C.: American Psychiatric Association, 1994.

Dietrich, Marlene. *Marlene*. New York: Grove Press, 1987.

Edwards, John. *Crossing Over: The Stories Behind the Stories*. 2001. San Diego: Jodere Group.

Flint, Leslie. *Voices in the Dark: My Life as a Medium*. London: Two Worlds, 2000.

Foy, Robin P. *In Pursuit of Physical Mediumship*. London: Janus Publishing Company, 1996.

Fulford, K. W. M. and Mike Jackson. *Philosophy, Psychiatry and Psychology*, "Spiritual Experience and Psychopathology," New York: Macmillan Publishing Company, 1969.

Guggenheim, Bill and Judy Guggenheim. *Hello From Heaven!* New York: Bantam Books, 1996

Hanut, Eryk. *I Wish You Love*. Berkeley: Frog, Ltd., 1966.

Jung, Carl. *Synchronicity: An Acausal Connecting Principle*. Princeton: Bollingen Series, Princeton University Press, 1973.

Kubler-Ross, Elisabeth. *The Wheel of Life: A Memoir of Living and Dying*. New York: Scribner, 1997.

Meyer, Marvin, Editor. *The Gospel of Thomas: The Hidden Sayings of Jesus*. San Francisco: Harper Collins, 1992.

Moody, Jr., Raymond A. *Reflections on Life After Life*. New York: Bantam Books, 1985.

Morse, Melvin. *Closer to the Light*. New York: Ivy Books, 1991.

Riva, Maria. *Marlene Dietrich*. New York: Alfred A. Knopf, Inc., 1992.

Schucman, Helen. *A Course in Miracles*. Glen Ellen, California: Foundation for Inner Peace, 1985.

Schwartz, G. E. and Russek, L. G. *The Living Energy Universe: A Fundamental Discovery that Transforms Science and Medicine*. Charlottesville: Hampton Roads Publishing (www.livingenergyuniverse.com), 1999.

Schwartz, G. E. and L. G. Russek. "Evidence of anomalous information retrieval between two research mediums: Telepathy, network memory resonance, and survival of consciousness," *Journal of the Society for Psychical Research*. 2001.

Shakespeare, William. *Hamlet*. Louis B. Wright, Virginia A. La Mar, Editors. New York: Washington Square Press, 1976.

Solomon, Grant, and Jane Solomon. *The Scole Experiment*. London: Piatkus, 1999.

————*A Basic Guide to the Development of Physical Psychic Phenomena Using Energy*. Norfolk, England: Spiritual Science Foundation.

Van Praagh, James. *Talking to Heaven*. New York: Penguin USA, 1999.

Weiss, Brian L. *Many Lives, Many Masters*. New York: Simon and Schuster Inc., 1988.

Weiss, Brian L. *Only Love is Real: A Story of Soulmates Reunited*. New York: Warner Books, 1996.

Notes

1. A "Sentient ADC": the Guggenheims refer to this "Sensing a Presence" experience as the most common type of ADC (Guggenheim, 21).

2. The Guggenheims describe this type of experience as a "Sleep-State" ADC, in which a person feels they have been contacted by a deceased loved one while asleep (Guggenheim, 125).

3. An "ADC of Physical Phenomena," these types of events are "unusual physical occurrences following the death of a relative or friend" regarded as contact with a deceased loved one (Guggenheims, 173).

4. Condor is a sister airline of Lufthansa.

5. The work of the Scole Group was later the focus of the British bestseller, *The Scole Experiment* by

Grant and Jane Solomon (Piatkus, 1999), which includes my firsthand account of this sitting.

6. The Scole Group have authored a "How To Do It" booklet entitled, *A Basic Guide to the Development of Physical Psychic Phenomena Using Energy*, and skeptics and interested parties are invited to replicate the experiment.

7. An investigation of the Scole Group was conducted by three members of the 115-year-old Society for Psychical Research in Great Britain (SPR); their report, which strongly advocated authenticity of some of Group's phenomena, was published in *Proceedings of the Society for Psychical Research*, Volume 58, Part 220, November 1999.

8. *A Course in Miracles*, Foundation for Inner Peace, 1985. The Course is a self-study program of spiritual psychotherapy which teaches the relinquishing of a thought system based on fear in exchange for a thought system based on love.

About the Author

Photo by Bill Keefrey

George E. Dalzell, L.C.S.W., is a graduate of Northwestern University. He holds a masters degree in social work and is licensed by the Board of Behavioral Science Examiners in the state of California (LCS 19150). He is employed by the Los Angeles County Department of Mental Health, as well as a Los Angeles area hospital. His writing is featured in the book, *The Scole Experiment* by Grant and Jane Solomon (Piatkus, 1999). He has appeared as a mental health expert on *LEEZA*, as well as on numerous radio shows, including *GOOD DAY U.S.A.* Public speaking engagements include a testimonial given before the British Society for Psychical Research in London in December 1999 at "The Scole Debate." He is a member of the Skeptics Society, and encourages the application of critical thinking.

The author is currently participating in mediumship research at the University of Arizona's Human Energy Systems Laboratory under the auspices of Gary E. Schwartz, Ph.D.

For more information regarding George Dalzell, see his website at: www.georgedalzell.com.

About Gary E. Schwartz, Ph.D.

Gary E. Schwartz, Ph.D. is professor of psychology, medicine, neurology, psychiatry, and surgery, and director of the Human Energy Systems Laboratory, at the University of Arizona. He received his Ph.D. from Harvard University in 1971 and was an assistant professor of psychology at Harvard until 1976. He was professor of psychology and psychiatry at Yale University, director of the Yale Psychophysiology Center, and co-director of the Yale Behavioral Medicine Clinic until 1988, when he moved to Arizona. He has published more than 300 scientific papers, including six papers in the journal *Science*. He has co-authored *The Living Energy Universe* (Hampton Roads, 1999) and *The Afterlife Experiments: Breakthrough Scientific Evidence of Life After Death*.

HAMPTON ROADS
PUBLISHING COMPANY, INC.
for the evolving human spirit

Thank you for reading Messages. Hampton Roads is proud to publish an extensive array of books on the topics discussed in this book, such as after-death communication and life after death. Please take a look at the following selection or visit us anytime on the web: www.hrpub.com.

Afterlife Encounters
Ordinary People, Extraordinary Experiences
Dianne Arcangel
Foreword by Gary E. Schwartz, Ph.D.

Dianne Arcangel, a former hospice worker and director of the Elisabeth Kübler-Ross Center, created the Afterlife Encounters Survey, a five-year, international survival study. *Afterlife Encounters* reveals the results of this landmark study, presenting not only the data, but also the stories beyond the numbers. Included are amazing stories of apparitions revealing who had murdered them; where family treasure was buried; even one spirit who provided a remarkable account of the tragedies of 9/11, weeks before those events occurred.

Paperback • 352 pages • ISBN 978-1-57174-436-4 • $15.95

Induced After-Death Communication
A New Therapy for Healing Grief and Trauma
**Allan L. Botkin, Psy.D.,
with R. Craig Hogan, Ph.D.**
Foreword by Raymond A. Moody, Jr., Ph.D., M.D.

Induced After-Death Communication is the inside story of a revolutionary therapy that will profoundly affect how grief and trauma are understood and treated. Botkin, a clinical psychologist, created the therapy while counseling Vietnam veterans in his work at a Chicago area VA hospital. Botkin recounts his initial— accidental—discovery of IADC during therapy sessions with Sam, a Vietnam vet haunted by the memory of a Vietnamese girl he couldn't save. During the session, quite unexpectedly, Sam saw a vision of the girl's spirit, who told him everything was okay; she was at peace now. This single moment surpassed months—years—of therapy, and allowed Sam to reconnect with his family.

Paperback • 224 pages • ISBN 978-1-57174-423-4 • $15.95

The Afterlife Codes
Searching for Evidence of the Survival of the Soul
Susy Smith

Is there a way to prove once and for all there is life after death? Prolific writer and psychic Susy Smith has spent her entire, long life searching for the technique, and now she says she's found it—the afterlife codes. In a charming, personable manner, Smith recounts her development as a psychic; her spiritual world contacts; the lasting friendship with her mother even after death; and the mistakes, doubts, and breakthroughs in her own quest to understand the "other side."

Paperback • 256 pages • ISBN 978-1-57174-191-2 • $14.95

Hampton Roads Publishing Company
. . . for the evolving human spirit

Hampton Roads Publishing Company
publishes books on a variety of subjects including
metaphysics, health, complementary medicine,
visionary fiction, and other related topics.

For a copy of our latest catalog,
call toll-free, 800-766-8009,
or send your name and address to:

Hampton Roads Publishing Company, Inc.
1125 Stoney Ridge Road
Charlottesville, VA 22902
e-mail: hrpc@hrpub.com
www.hrpub.com